HELL'S PROPHECY

THE SECOND DEATH

Steve Henderson

Copyright © 2025 by Steve Henderson

All rights reserved.

No part of this publication may be reproduced, distributed, or transmitted in any form or by any means, including photocopying, recording, or other electronic or mechanical methods, without the prior written permission of the publisher, except in the case of brief quotations embodied in critical reviews and certain other noncommercial uses permitted by copyright law.

ISBN:

The paperback is: 979-8-9924928-2-8

The Hardcover is: 979-8-9924928-1-1

The E-Book is 979-8-9924928-3-5

Dedication

This Book is dedicated to my two deceased sons:

Jason Henderson March 11, 1981- July 20, 2005

Jacob Henderson November 10, 1989 - October 20, 2022

"Good people pass away; the godly often die before their time. But no one seems to care or wonder why. No one seems to understand that God is protecting them from the evil to come." Isaiah 57:1 (NLT)

Acknowledgments

Thanks to my friends and family, who, over the years, have encouraged me to share my unique perspective on Hell in a Book. Special thanks to Mary Baxter and Bill Wiese for using quotes from their books.

A special thanks to NH Arafat for his help in making the book all it could be, thanks to his creative artistry on the book cover.

I want to extend a very special thank you to my friend and Brother, Mason Jones, for his contribution to making the publication of this book possible.

Above all, I thank my Lord and Savior for the profound inspiration to put these words into a book guided by His Spirit and to share these precious truths with those who seek them out.

Preface

Shortly after dedicating my life to God's purpose, my mother passed away from cancer. She never spoke about God and did not know Jesus, and she could not receive the gift of eternal life. Her death drove me to search the Bible for answers about her fate. What I found was deeply troubling. On the surface, it seemed that she was condemned to eternal torment and misery.

The idea of eternal fire was disturbing and shook my sense of peace with God. The concept of Hell contradicted Yahweh's Amazing Grace strikingly. How could this God of Love condemn my mother to endless torture? How could the lover of my soul become a vengeful tyrant, inflicting eternal pain on the woman who gave me life? Would the same Jesus, who suffered so much on the cross, turn around and condemn others to endless torment? It just did not add up.

The notion of eternal suffering felt so alien to me, so a few decades ago, seeking peace and clarity for my troubled mind, I started taking a deep look into the Scriptures to understand Hell. As I explored further, many straightforward statements about death and Hell did not make sense. It was like trying to make two plus two equal to five. Something about the "eternal Hell" doctrine did not sit right with me.

My in-depth study revealed a unique perspective that differs from the popular view of God's judgment in Hell. The Bible speaks of an "end" to the wicked, confirming that evil will end just as it had a beginning. This realization comforted me and brought a deeper understanding of my Maker's ultimate plan.

HELL'S PROPHECY

I am relieved to know that my mother will not be eternally tortured, suffering endlessly in a sulfuric inferno under the rule of the devil. God forbid.

I have read and examined the usual teachings about Hell. Recently, I delved into two books on the subject: the bestseller *"23 Minutes in Hell" and another titled "A Divine Revelation of Hell."* Both authors share their firsthand experiences of being given guided tours of Hell, and I was astonished and shocked by the details of the creatures in Hell:

"I will try to describe the looks of these evil beings. The one speaking was extensive, about the size of a full-grown grizzly bear, brown in color, with a head like a bat and eyes that were set very far back into a hairy face. Hairy arms fell to his sides, and fangs came out of the hair on his face. Another one was small like a monkey with very long arms and hair all over his body. His face was tiny, and he had a pointed nose. I could see no eyes on him anywhere... The sight of these demons and evil spirits, and the terrible odor that came from them, made me sick to my stomach."[1]

-Mary Baxter

Like the author, many Christians have depicted Hell in bizarre ways, trying to instill fear and promote following Jesus. However, this approach raises a crucial question: Can one truly comprehend a loving, merciful, kind, and forgiving God if the choice is between eternal life and unending misery? This traditional theology, I believe, is deeply unsettling.

One popular Bible teacher, the Bible Answer Man, claims that *"without Hell, there can be no salvation."*[2] But must there be a "Hell" to be saved? Does our salvation hinge on the fear of endless torture? This is a false assumption - quite the contrary.

Instead of believers facing the threat of burning in "God's Great Eternal Barbecue," sharing the message of Jesus' immense love in salvation makes much more sense. He gave His only Son

Preface

to die for us. This approach is a much more powerful attraction. Love's attraction will always surpass the fear of eternal punishment in motivating someone to respond.

"To love a god that would send another to a place of endless anguish is akin to pretend loving the schoolyard bully to prevent personal abuse... No human in sane control of their thought processes would send others to eternal punishment for any crime. Nor would they stand idly by allowing it to happen without protest of some kind." [3]

-David Nichols

Like this atheist, the concept of eternal torment has turned many people against God. The big question they ask is: How can a Loving God inflict eternal torture? After all, the Bible teaches us to be merciful, love our enemies, and treat others as we would want to be treated. Didn't Jesus, God with us, embody these principles during His time on Earth? So, where does Hell fit into these eternal truths? Can Hell and eternal bliss co-exist?

The teaching of Hell has led to more skeptics than believers. Could our Merciful God be a maniacal monster, spewing out hate for eternity? This doctrine paints God as a sadist. Even the renowned C.S. Lewis acknowledged that the doctrine of Hell is:

"One of the chief grounds on which Christianity is attacked as barbarous and the goodness of God impugned." [4]

Such a harsh concept will naturally elicit a harsh response from most folks.

Let us be clear: The prophecy of Hell warns us of an unstoppable fire. Yes – Vengeance comes from God, and the wicked will face their reward. There will be no second chances, and everything hidden will be brought to light. Justice is on its way. However, the Divine Judge takes *"no pleasure in the death* *of the wicked."*5 The Creator of Love does not wish for anyone to perish.

For those grappling with the complex topic of Hell, this exegesis seeks to demonstrate the harmony between God's love and His Righteous Judgment. The Bible's teachings on mercy and fairness are perfectly balanced. I aim to reveal the unfiltered biblical truth about this worrisome topic. In addition, I hope to comfort and liberate those who have struggled with the idea of an eternally angry God.

What is your perspective? Should evil be allowed to exist forever? Will the wicked be able to endure eternal torment? What exactly is the "Second Death," and will it end the madness and hatred in the universe? If people are already suffering in Hell, why would God need to resurrect them for a future Judgment?

These critical questions deserve rational, thoughtful answers, and engaging with them can lead to a deeper understanding of our faith.

Imagine a world where there is no more crying, pain, or sorrow. History has passed, and we have "a new Heaven and Earth" for the righteous to live in. No rapists, no thugs, no place for evil to continue.

Doesn't the idea of letting maniacs live forever seem unreasonable? For them, wouldn't "Hell" be bliss?

As you delve into this book, you will see that the modern notion of "Hell" is more myth than reality. This book will free many from the grip of fear. Discovering this truth will enable "perfect love to drive out fear" and dispel the myth, bringing relief and comfort to those troubled by the concept of eternal darkness.

Preface

May your love for God grow, and may the contents of this book bring you greater peace.

Steve Henderson

Evangelist/Apologist

Contents

Acknowledgments iv
Preface v
The Wrong Portrait 1
What the Hell? 9
New Testament Words Translated "Hell" 14
Rational Arguments Against Eternal Torture 19
The Sensationalism of Hell 28
The 'Living Dead' in Hell 32
Death's Sleep 37
Death's Inactivity 42
When the Hell? 48
Where the Hell? 52
Why the Hell? 62
The First Resurrection 69
How the Hell? 82
The Second Death 88
Hell No More 965
The Rich Man and Lazarus 1021
Hell No 1132
So – Are You Facing Bad News? 1255
Hell, With the Good News 1332
Here Is the Best News 1409
About the Author 1443
Reference 146

The Wrong Portrait

I firmly oppose the portrayal of the gospel as an ultimatum, where individuals are threatened with an everlasting Hell alongside the Devil and his demons. This is a flawed depiction of our God and Savior, Yahweh. I am committed to proving this point beyond any doubt.

This erroneous image of God is highly problematic. Imagine having a father who is physically abusive and threatens to burn you with a hot iron every time you step out of line. While you might respect him out of fear of being harmed, it is doubtful that you will love him with all your heart. The threat of torture is already bad enough, but the idea of it lasting forever? Come on – that is just inconceivable. Fear may elicit a response, but it will never reciprocate genuine love and respect.

To truly understand Yahweh, we must see Him as a Loving and Compassionate Father whose primary desire is to save and uplift, not to punish or instill fear. Only then can we respond with the love and reverence that He deserves. After all, it is God's Goodness, not psychotic portrayals of an insane deity, that will attract someone to respond positively. It is vital to understand *"that the kindness of God leads you to repentance." (Romans 2:4)*

We have often read or heard about heroic rescues that have ended in the rescuer's death. In our country, certain days are set aside to remember the brave heroes who gave their lives to bring us freedom. It is only right to honor those willing to make the ultimate sacrifice so that we may live in peace and security.

HELL'S PROPHECY

Because of their death and sacrifice, we continue to have the privilege of living happy and free lives.

When I was at Walter Reed Medical Center with my dying son, I met many soldiers who had lost their legs; wheelchairs were everywhere. These soldiers were proud to have given up their limbs so we could continue walking peacefully. Their sacrifices remind us of the profound cost of our freedom, recognizing the deep duty they felt toward protecting our way of life. We acknowledge our need to remember and appreciate those who have offered up their lives to keep us safe.

Now, imagine someone offering you a chance to live forever. The price for you is free. However, the One who offers such an incredible gift must die for you to receive it. This is because the Giver of such life loved you so immensely that: *"He gave up His Only Son, that whoever believes in Him would not perish, but have everlasting life" (John 3:16).* Let's get the picture straight.

No matter how often we have heard of this loving statement from Jesus, it still amazes us to ponder such an enormous commitment—to give up His Divine Glory, humble Himself, and then suffer death for our sake. How can anyone believe for a moment that this manifestation of Love and Glorious Grace could ever torture anyone without end? Dream on.

The Savior clearly articulated his goals: *"No greater love will you find than this—that a man lay down his life for his friends" (John 15:13).* To God, it was all about saving the objects of His love. *"For God did not send His Son into the world to condemn it, but that the world through Him might be saved" (John 3:17).*

It is vital to understand that Jesus' mission was not one of condemnation but of salvation. His intentions were purely born from immense Love, not malice. His self-sacrifice on the Cross was an ultimate act of Love, rescuing humanity from the grip of eternal death. His act of Great Mercy set us free from the chains of sin and evil, granting us the opportunity for salvation and eternal life. His goal was not punishment or retribution but offering us a path to redemption, demonstrating His boundless compassion toward us.

Think about the colossal imposition and enormous changes He had to implement to restore the lost and dead to Himself:

"Who, being in the form of God, did not consider it robbery to be equal with God, but made Himself of no reputation, taking the form of a bondservant, and coming in the likeness of men. And being found in appearance as a man, He humbled Himself and became obedient to the point of death, even death on a cross" (Philippians 2:6-8).

The cost that Jesus paid for our freedom was more than we can conceptualize:

"He was despised and abandoned by men, A man of great pain and familiar with sickness; And like one from whom people hide their faces, He was despised, and we had no regard for Him. However, it was our sicknesses that He bore and our pains that He carried, yet we assumed that He was afflicted, struck down by God, and humiliated. But He was pierced for our offenses; He was crushed for our wrongdoings; The punishment for our well-being was laid upon Him, And by His wounds, we are healed." (Isaiah 53:3-5)

Imagine the King of Kings stooping down, volunteering to suffer and go through such undeserved pain. The pure Lamb of Yahweh who laid down His Life:

"Consider Him who had endured such hostility by sinners against Himself...who for the joy set before Him, endured the cross, scorning its shame." (Hebrews 12:3a, 2b)

Yes, consider Him who suffered for us, consider Him who was despised and abandoned, consider Him who was struck down and humiliated, consider Him who carried our pain – and took on the death that we deserve, consider Him who was crucified and crushed because of our sin and rebellion, consider Him who committed no sin nor was any deceit in His Mouth, consider Him who made His Grave with the wicked. He gave up His Life as a ransom for us.

Why did the Son of God endure the unfair treatment that no man had witnessed? He did it because of the joy of knowing that one day, He would bring countless numbers back from the lost and dead. This is what He endured on the Cross for:

"A great multitude that no one could count, from every nation, tribe, people, and language, standing before the Throne and the Lamb. They were wearing white robes and were holding palm branches in their hands." (Revelation 7:9)

It is essential to understand that the focus of the Almighty was not on wrath but on the rescue of humanity. When speaking with Moses, God explained to him that He was:

"The Lord Yahweh, Merciful and Gracious, Longsuffering and abounding in goodness and truth, keeping mercy for thousands, forgiving iniquity and transgression and sin" (Exodus 34:6-7).

Our Merciful God came to rescue us from the power of evil's hold on us. Repeatedly, the Loving Creator pleaded with his people:

The Wrong Portrait

"As I live, I have no pleasure in the death of the wicked, but that the wicked turn from his way and live. Turn, turn from your evil ways! For why should you die?" (Ezekiel 33:11).

Portraying God as an angry tyrant who is just waiting to torture wicked people forever and ever is not who He is. Our Creator, who is *"longsuffering towards us," is not willing for any to perish but for all to come to repentance* (2 Peter 3:9).

His offer: eternal life or perish. It is our choice.

By the testimony of Scripture, we may conclude that *"God is Love;"* Love is not what God *has*, but what He *is*. Love will demonstrate its righteous actions in every way. Never will a threat to "turn or burn" bring anyone around to pure love. Quite the contrary. It is important to note that:

"Love consists of this: not that we loved God, but that He loved us and sent His Son as the Atoning Sacrifice for our sins." (1 John 4:10)

Initially, God created the Angels to commune with those He could love and dwell with. He saw no joy in creating robots programmed to love Him back. The Almighty Yahweh decided to give them a choice in the matter. They were created as free moral agents. This would be the only way love could be determined legitimate. It takes two to tango.

Love could not be forced. But in allowing His Creation to make their own minds up, God knew the risk involved in allowing free choice. At a specific time, one of the highest angels in Heaven exercised his freedom to rebel against his Maker. When Lucifer began to rebel, pride entered his heart and became the unfastening of a harmonious Creation.

HELL'S PROPHECY

It was the highest angel in Yahweh's Created Order who exercised His free will and introduced evil into the world. He began to get a big head. He had "I" trouble. The Scriptures provide us insight as to Satan's rebellion:

"How you have fallen from Heaven, O Lucifer, son of the morning! How you are cut down to the ground, you who weakened the nations! For you have said in your heart: 'I will ascend into heaven, I will exalt my throne above the stars of God; I will also sit on the mount of the congregation on the farthest sides of the north; I will ascend above the heights of the clouds, I will be like the Highest.' (Isaiah 14:12-14)

When evil infiltrated the world, shattering the perfect harmony of His Creation, decisive action was necessary to address the origin of this rebellion and to those who would follow the path of this malevolent angel. A plan was set in motion to create a realm where Satan could reign for a time.

The disillusioned angel could no longer tread upon the sacred fiery stones of Yahweh's Holy Mountain. Thus, the Almighty fashioned a place called Earth to serve as a testament to the unfallen universe, Lucifer's true intentions, and the consequences of aligning with this deranged angel.

As evil entered the world and subsequently brought rebellion into Yahweh's perfect Order, something had to be done with the metastasized cancer spreading across the universe. By crafting Earth, God provided a stage to demonstrate the stark reality of rebellion and the outcomes of following Lucifer's madness. Educating and protecting the rest of Creation was a profound and deliberate act.

The Wrong Portrait

Yahweh could have wiped out Lucifer instantly, but that would have elicited the wrong response in the unfallen world: worshiping Him out of fear instead of out of love.

"Love has been perfected among us in this: that we may have boldness in the Day of Judgment...There is no fear in love, but perfect love casts out fear because fear involves torment. But he who fears has not been made perfect in love." (1 John 4:17-18)

Here is my point: Throwing the threat of "eternal torture" in the face of the lost will never bring them to the place of perfect love. In other words, having an ideal love is difficult if you are scared.

Jesus declared:

"If I am lifted up from the Earth, all men will be drawn to me" (John 15:32).

According to Jesus, lifting love up would be the catalyst that draws the lost to God, not the terror of burning forever in a dark Hell.

Yeshua was tortured on a cruel instrument of pain for our sins. He died a death that did not belong to Him. He took on our death, in death's grip, for three days. He was raised from the dead, a victory over the grave. He did it to destroy the works of the Devil and reconcile us back from the death sentence to Himself. Yeshua died in the most horrific way to rescue us from the *Second Death.*

The teaching that portrays Yahweh as an insane God who will torture those who do not abide in His Love for trillions upon trillions of years - just does not square up with the old story of the Cross.

HELL'S PROPHECY

Yes - *"God demonstrated His Great Love for us that while we were sinners – Jesus died for us." (Romans 5:8)*

What the Hell?

"Hell has a body (like a human form) lying on her back in the center of the earth. Hell is shaped like a human body, very large and with many chambers of torment."

-Mary Baxter

The word "Hell" has woven deeply into our everyday language. It is common in conversations—I have even been told to go there a few times! People often say they've *"been through Hell"* or *"caught Hell"* for assorted reasons. This concept has fueled numerous horror films, such as *"Jason Goes to Hell"* and *"Hellraiser,"* conjuring images of a terrifying underworld where evil thrives. Movie producers have made millions by spinning these nightmarish tales of a fiery, torturous domain.

Many famous people have made quotes concerning their viewpoint of this place:

"To work hard, to live hard, to die hard, and then go to Hell after all would be too damn hard."[7]

-Carl Sandburg

Interestingly, there are three places where you can find Hell: 1) in Michigan, 2) in Norway, and 3) in the Cayman Islands. These are the only locations on the map where you will find "Hell." Surprisingly, two of the three Hells experience freezing temperatures during the winter. The Eagles, a rock band, even named an album 'Hell Freezes Over,' possibly inspired by these two frosty little havens in Michigan and Norway; besides these quirky towns, no other 'Hell' exists.

Some preachers claim to know its exact location, but perhaps they should first understand what the original word for "Hell" meant before drawing any conclusions.

Understanding the origins of words is crucial, especially when interpreting the Concept of Hell in the Bible. "Hell" did not exist in the original Greek and Hebrew texts. This revelation might surprise some, disappoint others, and even bring relief to a few.

Etymologists and theologians agree that "Hell" was absent in the original Scriptures. This term appeared centuries after the Holy Scriptures were translated from Hebrew and Greek. The origin of the word "Hell" can be traced back to the Old English term *"hel"* or *"helle,"* which referred to the *"underworld or the abode of the dead"* and conveyed meanings of *covering, concealing, or saving.* The English word may also partly derive from the Old Norse *"Hel,"* meaning *"one who covers up or hides something."*[8]

The earliest usage of "Hell" dates to around 725 A.D., long after the Hebrew and Greek Testaments were written. Over time, the concept of "Hell" as a place of eternal torment for the wicked evolved, influenced by different cultural and religious beliefs.

Through the centuries, the depiction of "Hell" has undergone significant transformations, shaped by various cultural, religious, and linguistic influences. Understanding its origins helps clarify how our concept differs from the original meanings and contexts.

The Hebrew Old Testament uses the word *"Sheol"* sixty-six times to describe the place of the dead. Interestingly, Jewish translations of the Hebrew Old Testament do not include the word "Hell" at all. Surprisingly, many Hebrew scholars dismiss the Christian interpretation of "Hell," noting that their Scriptures are entirely silent on the idea of eternal torture for the wicked.

It is important to note that the Hebrew word *"Sheol"* has been translated into three different terms in the modern Bible: *"Hell"* (thirty-one times), *"Grave"* (thirty-one times), and *"Pit"* (three times). Although the terms share the same original meaning, each carries a distinct interpretation.

A closer examination of the word *"Sheol"* in the Old Testament reveals passages where it is used to declare that the Messiah's soul would not remain in "Hell" after His death. For example, in a prophecy foretelling the Messiah's Resurrection, Psalm 16:10 prophesied:

"For thou wilt not leave my soul in Hell (Sheol); neither wilt thou suffer thine Holy One to see corruption."

Another prophecy, speaking of the same event and using the term "Sheol," states that the Messiah *"made His grave (Sheol) with the wicked" (Isaiah 53:9)*. This demonstrates that "Sheol" was used interchangeably to signify the grave or the realm of the dead. These revelations indicate that the Messiah would not remain in Sheol very long and would remain dead. Again, in this context, "Sheol" is considered a place associated with the grave.

Additionally, on a few occasions, "Sheol" is translated as *"pit."* For example, Isaiah 38:18 states:

"For Sheol cannot thank you, Death cannot praise you; those who go down to the pit (Sheol) cannot hope for your truth."

The concept of "Sheol" throughout the Scriptures emphasizes the separation from life and the cessation of earthly existence, rather than remaining alive *"roasting and toasting"* in a bottomless pit. The modern concept of "Hell" is far removed from its original intent.

Another Old Testament passage describes *"Sheol"* as a place where:

"Like sheep, they are appointed for Sheol; death shall be their shepherd, and the upright shall rule over them in the morning. Their form shall be consumed in Sheol, with no place to dwell." (Psalm 49:14)

In this land of the dead, the deceased is *"consumed,"* leaving no living presence there - no hollering curses, no screaming in pain, no weeping, no teeth grinding.

In another passage, Yahweh declared:

"A fire is kindled in My Anger, and shall burn to the lowest Hell (Sheol), it shall consume the Earth... devoured by pestilence and bitter destruction that consumes the planet. (Deuteronomy 32:22,24)

"Sheol," translated as "Hell," is associated with total obliteration. "Hell" devours and consumes its victims. The terms *"consume,"* *"devour,"* and *"destruction"* in this context signify an *"end"* to evil. Again, there is not one hint of eternal conscious torment - not once.

Another Bible writer proclaimed:

"Hell (Sheol) and Destruction are before Yahweh" (Proverbs 15:11). Those who end up in this unfortunate place face destruction. Repeatedly, the Old Testament links "Hell" with death and *"destruction"* without any indication of eternal burning. Everything associated with "Sheol" leads to ruin and finality.

What the Hell?

Here is an eye-opening epiphany from the Prophet Ezekiel:

"They have all been delivered to death, to the depths of the Earth, among the children of men who go down to the pit… to Hell together with those who descend to the Pit." (Ezekiel 31:14,16)

Based on the Prophet's words, "Sheol" will be a place where those who arrive there are comforted in the depths of the earth *(Ezekiel 31:16).*

There are no indications that the "*pit*" is a place of torment; instead, it is depicted as a place of **"comfort."** Ironically, the Old Testament reveals that good and bad people end up in "Sheol."

One final thought before we move on: Many theologians assert that "Hell" is a place where the wicked are eternally separated from God. However, a close examination of the word "*Sheol*" in this passage of Psalm 139:8 suggests otherwise:

"Though I make my bed in Hell (Sheol), behold, You are there."

If Yahweh can be present in "Hell," how can anyone be eternally separated from His Presence?

The theology of "Hell" appears to have many loopholes. One thing is sure - nothing can separate us, nor hide us from the Almighty, when He decides to show up there!

New Testament Words Translated "Hell"

"**H**ell" is translated from two primary Greek words in the New Testament. The first is *"Gehenna,"* which refers to Israel's *"Valley of Hinnom."* The word "Gehenna" is rendered as "Hell" eleven times in the New Testament. This term refers to a literal, historical location in a valley outside the walls of Jerusalem. In the Old Testament, the Israelites sacrificed their children in this valley, linking it to many tragic events.

The *Valley of Hinnom* was also a garbage dump where all of Israel's trash was burned. Jesus used this site as a metaphor to illustrate the fate of the wicked. The fire in the dump was always burning, but nothing could survive in it for long. In this context, *"Hell"* (*Gehenna*) referred to a specific place *above the ground*, not at the center of the Earth.

The Old Testament references this location as:

"The Valley of Slaughter, for they will bury the dead in Topheth until there is no more room. The corpses will become food for the birds of the air and the beasts of the Earth... "They shall not be gathered or buried; they shall be dung upon the face of the Earth, and death shall be chosen rather than life." (Jeremiah 7:32-33; 8:2,3)

In the Old Testament, the valley of Hinnom (*Gehenna*) is pictured as a place of massacre, where dead bodies would be scattered across the ground. In the New Testament, Jesus frequently referred to this place when discussing the fate of the wicked. Repeatedly, death metaphors appear, but none of these verses suggest endless torture. Instead, "Hell" is described as a valley of massacre where the wicked are killed and devoured.

Jesus likened *"Gehenna"* as a metaphor to warn that the people who choose to sin and rebel would one day be thrown into the garbage dump of Gehenna:

"And if your hand causes you to sin, cut it off; it is better for you to enter life maimed than having your two hands, to go into Hell (Gehenna), into the unquenchable fire." (Mark 9:43)

Interestingly, Jesus never implied that this place was beneath the Earth's surface. *Gehenna* then represented something vastly different from the modern concept of "Hell" preached by fire-and-brimstone preachers today. Those who heard Yeshua's warnings about being cast into *Gehenna* had an entirely different perspective.

The next word translated as "Hell" was *"Hades."* There was no equivalent Greek word for the Hebrew term "Sheol." The Greeks believed in the immortal soul and that everyone is alive in *"Hades,"* which led to the subtle emergence of the idea that the dead in Sheol are also alive. This notion transformed *Sheol* from a final resting place to a hot spot.

Consequently, this belief in immediate life after death influenced the translation of "Hell" from *"Hades."* The word *"Hades"* has its roots in Greek mythology.

Here is what *The Myth Encyclopedia* explains about the fable of *Hades*:

"The Greek underworld was divided into three regions: Hades, Tartarus, and Elysium. Most of the dead went to the kingdom of the god Hades. In the deepest part of the underworld, a terrible

*dark place known as Tartarus, the very wicked suffered eternal punishment at the hands of the Furies. The third region, Elysium or the Elysian Fields, was where exceptionally good and righteous people went after death."*9

Interestingly, the King James translators struggled to define *"Hades."* For instance, one verse in Revelation uses *"Hell"* in the main text, but *"grave"* in the margin. This pattern appears in other New Testament passages, where the translators could interpret the word either way. While the terms are often used interchangeably, they convey two distinct concepts in modern Christianity. At the Judgment, *Hades* will be thrown into the *"Lake of Fire"*:

"The sea gave up the dead in it, and Death and Hades gave up the dead in them, and each person was judged according to what they had done. Then Death and Hades were thrown into the Lake of Fire. The Lake of Fire is the Second Death." Revelation 20:13-14

According to the quoted Scripture, *Hades* holds the dead and, one day, it will release them for resurrection and judgment. After the judgment, *Hades* will be thrown into the *Lake of Fire*. Those who were in Hades will face a *Second Death*. Note: Hades is not the same as the Lake of Fire. More on this will be covered in another chapter.

Additionally, one more word is translated as "Hell" in the New Testament, appearing only once in the Bible. *"Tartaroo"* originates from the root "Tartaros" and is associated with the god *Hades*. In Greek mythology, *"Tartaros"* was considered the bottomless abyss of *Hades*. It was an underground realm and a place of eternal torment.

If "Hell" is a literal place, how did this term evolve from the ancient Hebrew word "Sheol" into an English word intertwined with mythological concepts? Why do the Jewish Scriptures remain silent on this *"hellhole"* in the Old Testament? Most translations have discarded the word because they acknowledge that "Hell" does not align with the original idea of the place of death. It is crucial to grasp this context.

In History, "Hell" gained widespread popularity thanks to Dante Alighieri's work "*Divina Commedia*," written around 1300 A.D. In this story, Dante and his guide, Virgil, journey through the Inferno and ascend the mountain of Purgatory. Virgil, being a virtuous pagan, was not condemned to Hell but was instead confined to Limbo, situated just at the edge of Hell.

In this poetic work, "Hell" is vividly detailed with nine concentric circles descending into its various depths, culminating in the very center where Satan is found, trapped in a frozen lake. From there, a small tunnel leads Dante and his guide, Virgil, on a journey through the Inferno and up Purgatorio Mountain.

Virgil, a virtuous pagan, was not condemned to Hell but confined to Limbo, situated just at the edge of Hell, on the other side of the world, at the Mountain of Purgatory. Remarkably, some religious groups adhere to this depiction.

An excerpt from Dante's Inferno describes it this way:

"Here sighs and lamentations and loud cries were echoing across the starless air so that, as soon as I [Dante] set out, I wept. Strange utterances, horrible pronouncements, accents of anger, words of suffering, and voice shrill and faints, and beating hands."[10]

-The Third Canta

New Testament Words Translated "Hell"

The word "Hell" comes from fables, not facts. Modern-day *"hellfire and brimstone"* preachers seem unaware that this term did not exist in the original Scriptures. Many Christians have adopted the belief that a *"place of the underworld"* actually exists, replacing truth with mythological legend. The Bible must be examined by its original words and intent. So, is there a place where people are burning now? ***"Hell" no!***

Rational Arguments Against Eternal Torture

The doctrine of eternal torment is often seen as a demonic slander that fosters widespread unbelief. At its core, this teaching suggests that Yahweh would choose to perpetuate evil. If death were not enough, the Loving Creator is presented as turning up the fire below, burning, scalding, and torturing those who did not know Him with horror tactics that would make Charles Manson look like a saint. Trillions and trillions of years without end, filled with the most unimaginable horror, all perpetrated in the name of justice.

This horrendous portrayal of a sane Deity, gone insane, has led many to hardened skepticism. This perspective contradicts the very character of a Loving and Just God. If God genuinely cared, would He subject His Creations to endless agony? One such cynic shares his slant on Hell and rationalism:

"I mean, guys, compare that 'God' with the worst monsters you can think of - Adolph Hitler, Joe Stalin, that sort of guy. None of them ever inflicted more than finite pain on their victims. The idea that the Mind of Creation (if such exists) wants to torture some of its critters for endless infinities of infinities seems too absurd to take seriously. Such a deranged Mind could not create a mud hut, much less the exquisitely mathematical universe around us."[11]

-Robert Anton Wilson

Reflect on the tragedy of a young sixteen-year-old who, after dying in a car wreck on prom night while drinking, must now endure an eternity of suffering. The sudden death is a profound loss enough, but to then imagine this youth cast into a pit of torture forever, terrorized by grotesque demons 24/7? This defies the very essence of Justice.

This concept of endless punishment for a momentary lapse of reason raises significant questions about God's Grace and Mercy. Does this extreme portrayal align with the character of a Loving and Just Creator?

Consider this preacher's view of "Hell" in his bizarre rant:

"We are terrified when we hear of executioners-scourging men, disjointing them, dismembering, tearing them in pieces, burning them with plates of red-hot metal. But these things are but a jest, a shadow compared with the torments of the next life."[12]

- Rev. Orby Shipley

The imagery described here is intense and terrifying. This belief depicts Yahweh as irrational, hateful, and vindictive. It seems perverse and insane to imagine a Loving God who would administer unjust punishments so harshly. The portrayal of Hell's eternal torture chamber constitutes *cruel and unusual punishment*, which is an apparent contradiction to the true essence of Divine Love and justice. Can a Just and Compassionate Deity eternally deep fry those who reject Him and choose another path for their life?

Cruel and unusual punishment refers to unfair treatment deemed unacceptable because of the *"suffering or humiliation it inflicts on the condemned person."* These noble principles first appeared in the English Bill of Rights in 1689 A.D. It is defined as follows:

"No one shall be subjected to torture or to cruel, inhuman, or degrading treatment or punishment."[13]

Around the globe, standards have been established against *"inhuman or degrading treatment or punishment."* Humanity acknowledges and agrees that there are limits to how justice should be administered. Our courts, law enforcement, and judicial systems have set parameters to ensure fairness and impartiality. Justice is measured and applied with fair treatment for all under its authority.

Some lines must not be crossed when implementing a just punishment. While castration might deter many sex offenders, it falls under *cruel and excessive* enforcement. If finite humans can comprehend and set such guidelines, it stands to reason that the Infinite Creator would model those principles at a much higher level of integrity. Common sense would assume this.

Furthermore, most believe God's justice will surpass human justice in terms of fairness and compassion. In His wisdom, He would embody the ultimate standard of Justice that balances mercy with righteousness, far more than the *"justice for all"* in our land.

The United States has established specific guidelines in the Constitution's Eighth Amendment to determine what constitutes *"cruel and unusual"* punishment. In 1972, Supreme Court Justice Brennan articulated:

"There are four principles by which we may determine whether a particular punishment is 'cruel and unusual.'[14]

According to the Supreme Court, the four determining factors of what constitutes *cruel and unusual* punishment are:

1) Punishment must not, by its severity, degrade human dignity, especially involving torture.

Rational Arguments Against Eternal Torture

This guideline emphasizes the importance of maintaining human dignity and preventing any form of torture, ensuring that justice is carried out with fairness and nobility.

To sentence someone to death is one thing, but torturing them crosses the line into indignity, far beyond what is a necessary payment for the crime committed. Even ten seconds of torture would be enough to change most people's attitudes. Imagine, then, ten trillion years of excruciating pain in Hell—and that is only the beginning of suffering with no end? Really?

What purpose would it serve for the executioner to continue killing once the condemned has died? One pull of the switch is sufficient. Ten seconds in a fire would likely be fatal to anything living. Indeed, being trapped in a fiery inferno for five minutes would reduce the body to a skeletal form. Once past the skeletal form, what is the sense? Why punish someone in a fire for more than a day or two? That is nonsense, not God's sense.

One atheist shares his view on the vulgar concept of God's cruel and unusual punishment of the wicked:

"Hell is an outrage on humanity. When you tell me that your deity made you in his image, I reply that he must have been very ugly."

- Victor Hugo

Despite Hitler's evil, even he understood that torturing a lifeless body was pointless once the enemy was dead. Now, imagine Jesus, who preached: *"Blessed are the merciful, for they shall obtain mercy"*—inflicting eternal torture on those who missed eternal life and keeping those souls alive in a scalding fire forever. This seems exceptionally irrational.

I could never endlessly torture people, especially my own children. How can anyone believe that Yahweh would do this to

His Children? This idea is hideous, portraying Yahweh as more monstrous than Hitler, instead of a loving Father who would even die for His enemies.

2) *A severe punishment inflicted in a wholly arbitrary fashion.*

There are clear parameters that distinguish right from wrong. The term "*arbitrary*" is characterized by making willful and often unwise or irrational choices. Punishing someone without first being accused and found guilty is an example of acting arbitrarily. This would be regarded as foolish.

For example, it is blatantly wrong for a court to sentence a person to death for jaywalking. To pronounce torture as punishment for someone crossing the road illegally would be considered both "*cruel and excessive*" by anyone's standards. Call it what it is: irrational and *wholly arbitrary*.

The concept of Hell extends far beyond a death sentence; it preserves the dead body and subjects it to *endless* execution. This notion is ludicrous. Supreme Intelligence will ultimately silence evil and eradicate the source of wicked intent.

The Bible declares the fate of the wicked: *"Into smoke, they shall vanish away" (Psalm 37:20).* Rather than perpetual torment, the wicked are depicted as *vanishing like smoke*, implying a complete and utter end to their existence. Ultimate justice involves the eradication of evil, not its endless perpetuation. Yahweh's Justice is absolute, providing a fitting *conclusion* to the existence of wickedness. Evil must come to an end.

3) *A severe punishment that is clearly rejected throughout society.*

Some will cut a head off to enforce Sharia Law. Others have found the guillotine to be quite expedient in the past. The reason that most civilized societies shun beheading is because of the heinous nature of the execution. In some countries, thieves are punished by cutting their hands off if caught. Although these may be significant crime deterrents, most people do not consider them humane and reject the severity of the punishment.

Emerging from the horrors of the Holocaust and the war crimes revealed during the Nuremberg trials, global leaders convened to reaffirm the Geneva Convention's standards of humane treatment. These standards were ratified by most of the civilized world and addressed grave breaches such as:

-Willful killing.
-Torture - inhumane treatment, including biological experiments.
*-Willfully causing great suffering or serious injury to the body or health.*15

Humanity cries out "no" to this cruelty. Just as the Geneva Conventions established a framework for humane treatment in the aftermath of unimaginable atrocities, if our human moral code of justice appears just, wouldn't the God who inscribed His Laws on stone with His Finger embody an even higher standard of justice and mercy?

Think about it: would it be rational for a righteous Judge to subject an unbelieving person who battled cancer for most of their life to eternal torture? What purpose would such a retribution serve? It seems fundamentally contrary to a Loving and Just Creator to inflict endless suffering. Divine retribution is about eradicating evil, not perpetuating suffering.

4) *Severe punishment is patently unnecessary.*

Most everyone would agree that prolonging the suffering of a death row inmate after execution would be senseless. No court in the world would agree to this heinous retribution for the offender.

HELL'S PROPHECY

The gas chamber and the electric chair are old relics that have been almost eliminated because they are regarded as instruments of *"cruel and unusual"* punishment. Some may disagree with how a person should die, but the courts have determined both "the chair" and "the gas chamber" as cruel instruments of death.

Now, in many states, there are concerns that even lethal injections are inhumane. There are even many debates now on whether a murderer should receive a death sentence. Many want to banish executions for good.

Life for life seems most equitable. Anything beyond that would be considered cruel and excessive in our land. In most places, euthanasia and abortion even cross the limits of tolerance in our standard of justice, imposing on man a tricky moral dilemma to resolve.

If humanity can legislate specific moral guidelines so as not to cross over, surely the King of Kings, the Lord of Lords, who legislated His Moral Law, will do the right thing when payback comes. It is sure that when the death sentence is conducted, it is by Our Savior, who is:

"Maintaining love to thousands, and forgiving wickedness, rebellion, and sin. Yet He does not leave the guilty unpunished." (Exodus 34:7)

Changing temporal sinners into immortal sinners for punishment is preposterous! There are no reasons for Yahweh to immortalize evil. Jesus came to take away sin, not to prolong it forever. The Prophet Zephaniah foretold of a time in which the Lord would:

"Take away Judgment, casting out the enemy, and evil would be seen no more." (Zephaniah 3:15)

Rational Arguments Against Eternal Torture

At some point in time, Yahweh declares:

"I am Merciful and will not keep My Anger forever." (Jeremiah 3:12)

What purpose would it serve for the God of Peace to kindle His Wrath throughout the endless ages? One would have to be forever angry to torture forever – you think? Would this not constitute cruel and unusual punishment, even in the most finite minds? One day, evil will be *"seen no more."*

"Hell" characterizes God as an angry psychopath who will never forgive. To be unforgiving means never letting someone who offends you off the hook. A forgiving person does not harbor hatred and hold onto anger, but enables the offense against them to be forgotten. Following the idea of forgiveness to its fullest extent makes excellent sense. At the heart of love and healing is forgiveness, received or applied.

I oppose the modern concept of "Hell" in Yahweh's Justice because there is no room to emulate forgiveness in this picture. In the heart of Yeshua, as he was hanging there dying our death for us, He asked forgiveness for those who were torturing Him. Would forgiveness then turn around and torture the ones forever who *"knew not what they were doing"*? *(Luke 23:34)*

Isn't life tough enough? Consider the natural disasters, war, poverty, cancer, pain, and tragedies that life dishes out. How can one, after coming to the time when their teeth fall out and the heart stops, deserve any more than death, let alone suffer eternal torture? Where does one find equity and even-handedness in perpetuating misery without end?

The sane mind rationalizes the concept of "Hell" with contempt. Even preachers are finding out that preaching more about the cross and what that means to humanity is much more

HELL'S PROPHECY

effective in reaching the hardened heart for Jesus than trying to scare the "Hell" into someone to believe!

The Sensationalism of Hell

"There is neither limit nor termination of these torments. There, the intelligent fire burns the limbs and restores them. It feeds on them and nourishes them."[16]

- Mark Minucius Felix

Over the years, I have heard many strange sermons about Hell that seem to contradict clear Biblical teachings on the subject. After reading numerous theologians' descriptions of the damned, I am convinced that many preachers exaggerate their concepts of Hell to the point of absurdity. Anyone can search from Genesis to Revelation and find no hint of Divine Justice being carried out in the dramatic ways some preachers depict.

According to this theologian's crazy view of the afterlife for the wicked, not only do a person's arms and legs burn endlessly, but they are also restored and nourished by this *"intelligent fire."* The rational mind struggles to conceive or grasp a fire that nourishes and restores anything it touches. Is there any verse in the Bible that supports this sensationalistic view of Hell?

Here is another example of profound depravity that exceeds rationality. A preacher illustrates how a child will suffer in Hell in this way:

"Little child, if you go to Hell, there will be a devil at your side to strike you. He will go on striking you every minute forever and ever without stopping. The first stroke will make your body as bad as the body of Job, covered, from head to foot, with sores and ulcers...

HELL'S PROPHECY

How, then, will your body be after the devil has been striking it every moment for a hundred millions of years without stopping."[17]

- The Sight of Hell (A Catholic book for children)

Not once does the Bible mention such a satanic treatment against children. Somewhere along the line, the writer of this twisted picture of terror toward a child had to be inspired by the Devil himself. What I find beyond bizarre is that many delight in portraying our Loving, Compassionate Savior in this way. The evil one gloats over his persuasion, convincing many to believe in such a perverted picture of Yahweh's Execution of Justice.

Blatant sensationalism has been connected to many of the "fire and brimstone" preachers throughout history. Hundreds of years ago, one minister exclaimed:

"The saints in heaven will be blessed by the view of the damned's misery, doubling their love and gratitude." [18]

The late *"Hellfire"* preacher Jonathan Edwards taught that the saints in heaven would increase their love for God as they witnessed their own eternal suffering. What kind of person, in their right mind, would rejoice in the torturous agony of anyone?

Consider this stretch of imagination depicting Hell:

"Beasts with spooky eyes and razor-sharp fangs tear into human flesh. Other mutant creatures rip bodies apart or plunge their own body parts right through abdomens and, backs and mouths. A black bird with ram horns uses its beak to puncture a man's face. Grotesqueries devour a person through a mouth where its stomach should be or use spiky limbs to drag people into eternal damnation."[19]

- Stephen Travels

Underneath the surface of this horror-filled picture is the heart of an unheard evil imagination conjured up by the mind of deep depravity. Where did this inspiration come from? I can tell you that this revelation of "Hell" did not come from the Biblical view of Sheol. Even the most horror-filled, satanic-inspired movies ever made pale in comparison! Where did his wisdom originate from?

Here is a Biblical answer:

"This wisdom descends not from above, but is earthly, sensual, and devilish. But the wisdom that is from above is first pure, then peaceful, gentle, and easy to be entreated." (James 3:15)

Another sensationalist shares his twisted concept of Satan's torture chamber in Hell in this way:

"There, damned souls roar without pity; gluttons are fed with toads and adders; burning oil is poured down the drunkard's throat; the usurer is forced to sup whole draughts of molten gold. The murderer is forever stabbed - yet can never die. The wanton lies on racks of burning steel, feeling the torment of his raging lust in his soul. There stand those wretched beings who have dreamt out whole years in lawless sheets and secret incest, cursing one another."

- Robert Southey

Where in the Bible does a diligent student of Scripture find such a bizarre illustration of such deep deviance? When the poet envisioned the *"murderer forever stabbed,"* he must not have read the Scripture that declares:

"No murderer has eternal life abiding in him." (1 John 3:15)

Wouldn't Jack the Ripper have the time of his eternal life in this environment? Just imagine slicing and dicing without any restraints, enjoying stabbing others lifeless with an unlimited number of victims to stalk. This thinking inspires producers for the next best-selling horror flick, *"Friday the 13th - Forever*

Stabbed." This kind of satanic fantasy makes millions at the box office.

And when we think the statements and imaginations about Hell cannot get any weirder, check this one out:

"I saw a soul in the form of a skeleton, crying, "Jesus have mercy." "Decayed flesh hung by shreds from her bones, and as it burned, it fell off into the bottom of the pit."[21]

- Mary Baxter

These outlandish claims about "Hell's" inhabitants must be rigorously examined against the Word of Truth. Where in the Scriptures does one find a soul depicted as a skeleton? How can there be decaying flesh on a soul? You can search the Bible day and night and not find a single verse linking a soul to a skeleton. How long do you think flesh could remain on a skeleton in God's Consuming Fire?

Many believers have chosen to believe in the myth of Hell as a place filled with creepy creatures, two-horned demons, spiders, snakes, and a torture chamber at the Earth's core. One can search the Bible high and low and not find such strange descriptions of a so-called Hell anywhere.

It is time to seriously examine why people exaggerate and sensationalize this dreadful concept of God's Eternal Torture Chamber. Does anyone believe that these depictions of satanic abuse and horror are part of Yahweh's Plan to eradicate evil? Really? Well, there are still some folks who think we came from monkeys. This is just a horrible perversion of the actual truth.

The 'Living Dead' in Hell

"I was standing in the middle of a cave...As I looked at the walls; I saw they were covered with thousands of hideous creatures. These demonic creatures were all sizes and shapes. Some of them had four legs and were the size of bears. Others stood upright and were about the size of gorillas. They were all terribly grotesque and disfigured...They seemed to me to be the living dead."[22]

- 23 Minutes in Hell

Remember, the deception began in the Garden. The father of lies attempted to deny death. Lucifer claimed, *"You won't really die."* After all, no one had witnessed death up to that point. Death was an unfamiliar concept, something Satan denied and scoffed at.

However, it did not take long to see who was telling the truth. The deceiver suggested to Eve that Yahweh did not understand and was mistaken when He warned Adam and Eve about death. To die or not to die—that was the core issue in evil's challenge to the Almighty's Authority. And so, it remains: do you die or not?

Many believe that when a wicked man dies, he goes straight to Hell. This means he moves to a *"hot spot,"* implying that death is not truly the end, but rather just a change of location, evading death's grip instantly.

In a split second, a person shuts their eyes and dies, and the next thing they know, they find themselves in an underworld as hot as molten iron, tormented with the *living dead* throughout eternity. It is an eerie notion. Nothing truly ends—people make a "swift shift" to another location.

Many horror movies play on this theme. Remember the popular television series "The *Walking Dead*"? It is based on the idea that the dead are not really dead. Horror flicks often depict mummies and zombies roaming around, alive but dead, trying to scare the devil out of people. Vampires also fit into this strange idea of immortal wickedness.

Today, many people believe that death is not the end of life, but rather a transition to a "*living dead*" state. In Christianity, this means going to Hell or Heaven. Other traditions incorporate concepts such as "*Purgatory*" or "*Limbo.*"

This belief that death is not truly the end of living contradicts Scripture and mocks God. According to this theology, death is not death; the wicked are not genuinely dead but just separated from God. This implies that the wicked have immortality.

Let's face it: the dead do die. Countless Bible verses and graveyards confirm this fact. How can anyone deny their mortality? What would be the purpose of dying if it did not indeed happen? Would there be a need for resurrection in this line of reasoning? Doesn't the Bible speak of being *raised from the dead?*

Immortality, by definition, is not subject to death. Despite numerous Scriptures opposing the idea of the wicked living forever, death is still viewed as transitional rather than final. For some reason, people hesitate to accept that death signifies a cessation of life.

Concerning the *"living dead,"* One Christian woman described her guided tour with Jesus into Hell and explained what she saw:

The 'Living Dead' in Hell

"The cries of the living dead, mixed with moans and hideous screams, came to my ears from all directions. There were no quiet times in Hell. The smell of dead and decaying flesh hung thickly in the air."[23]

- A Divine Revelation of Hell

This author described those in Hell as *"the living dead."* So, which is it: living or dead? Can the two co-exist? Can death live, too? The *"living dead"* concept makes as much sense as a vegetarian snorting methamphetamine. Some things do not mix.

As a teacher and minister, I have learned that every "vision" should be tested against specific Biblical criteria. There seems to be a Biblical contradiction in this writer's testimony about her visit to Hell. Nowhere in the Bible will you find the phrase *"living dead."*

Terms like *"hateful loving," "hairy baldness," "blindsight,"* and *"dry rain"* are other oxymorons that seem just as bizarre and senseless.

In the book *"23 Minutes in Hell,"* the author vividly describes Hell. Under the subheading *"The Living Dead,"* he wrote:

"I knew that most people on the surface of the earth did not believe or even know that there was an entire world going on down here. I was horrified by the deafening screams of untold multitudes of people crying out in torment... In Hell, there is no life of any kind. All is dead."

-Bill Weise

Reading such a testimony could confuse someone about the status of those in Hell. If *"all are dead"* and *"there is no life of any kind,"* are those in the underworld alive or dead as they scream out in torment?

The concept of a *"living dead"* person is difficult to grasp. Do the dead just appear to be alive? When the author reported, *"They seem to me to be the living dead,"* he seemed uncertain about the status of those "living dead."

Other religions also embrace the idea of "no death" scenarios. For instance, one belief based on reincarnation suggests that a person might transition into another form without dying, like transitioning into a frog; there is no actual death, just a change in status and position. These teachings stem from Lucifer's original lie about not dying.

Death is defined as the *"termination, a permanent cessation of all vital functions."* When an employer terminates someone for stealing, there is no return to that job. The term *"exterminate"* shares the same root. When a bug is exterminated, it dies. If a person's heart, kidneys, and lungs stop functioning, the body cannot revive. The very definition of *"death"* signifies termination. Yet, for some reason, many believe death is merely a separation, not the end of life.

It is important to note that immortality is granted only to those who embrace the gospel*:*

"But it has now been revealed through the appearing of our Savior, Christ Jesus, who has destroyed death and has brought life and immortality to light through the gospel" (2 Timothy 1:10).

For unbelievers, immortality is not possible - period.

Time and again, the Apostle Paul spoke of the fate of those who are saved and those who perish, of *"death unto death"* and *"life unto life" (2 Corinthians 2:15-16).*

In his understanding, a person faces one of two destinies. His theology offers no hint of the wicked living on forever. Death will ultimately meet its end. According to Scripture:

The 'Living Dead' in Hell

"The last enemy to be destroyed is death."

(1 Corinthians 15:26)

Even death itself will be *destroyed*. Yes – one day, there will be no such thing as death anymore. The enemies of God will be eliminated in the Fire Lake at the Second Death.

Death's Sleep

Contrary to popular belief, a person does not go to a Hell ruled by hatred immediately after death. Instead, they enter a state of "*sleep.*"

The Word of God confirms that Yeshua viewed death as a "sleep." When His friend Lazarus died, Jesus said, *"Our friend Lazarus has fallen asleep; but I am going, so that I may awaken him from sleep" (John 11:11).*

Yeshua's disciples initially misunderstood this metaphor, thinking He meant natural sleep. However, He spoke to them plainly, *"Lazarus is dead" (John 11:12-13).* To Jesus, death was akin to sleep, and Lazarus awoke from this sleep after four days.

The same will occur at the Resurrection. Yeshua will call forth those who are "sleeping," and they will rise from their graves.

Paul frequently likened death to a "sleep." He foretold, *"We shall not all sleep, but we shall all be changed" (1 Corinthians 15:51).* He also said, *"Then those also who have fallen asleep in Christ have perished" (1 Corinthians 15:18).*

Paul mentioned some five hundred witnesses who saw Jesus after His Resurrection—some were still alive when he wrote his testimony, while others had *"fallen asleep."* (1 Corinthians 15:6)

Interestingly, Paul, who wrote many letters in the New Testament, never mentioned Hell even once. His writings did not hint at a *"death to Hell"* concept. He understood death, both for good and evil, as a "sleep." He never suggested that Hell was full of angry sinners. To the contrary:

"I do not want you to be ignorant, brethren, concerning those who have fallen asleep, lest you sorrow as others who have no hope." (1 Thessalonians 4:13)

According to this revelation, we are not to be ignorant about the dead - the condemned are not in "Hell," nor are there any "living dead" there. They are simply sleeping in their graves, waiting for their appointed time to come. When the time comes, they will hear the voice of God and rise from the ground to receive their due reward.

Paul eagerly anticipated his reward, proclaiming,

"There is laid up for me a crown of righteousness which the Righteous Judge shall give me at that Day, and not to me only, but unto all of them that love His Appearing." (2 Timothy 4:8)

His ultimate focus was on the prize: *"that he might attain to the resurrection from the dead" (Philippians 3:11).* Paul knew he would die and prayed to be found worthy of a resurrection from death's hold someday.

Paul's theology presented death as a peaceful sleep for the saints awaiting their reward from the grave. This biblical concept gave rise to the phrase *"rest in peace."* Through this analogy, Paul emphasized the temporary nature of death, much like sleep, with the expectation of a bodily resurrection:

"Behold, I tell you a mystery: We shall not all sleep, but we shall all be changed— in a flash, in the twinkling of an eye, at the Last Trumpet. The Trumpet will sound, the dead will be raised imperishable, and we will be changed."

"This corruption must put on incorruption, and this mortal must put on immortality. So, when this corruptible has put on incorruption, and this mortal has put on immortality, then shall be brought to pass the saying that is written: "Death is swallowed up in victory." (1 Corinthians 15:51-54)

It is essential to grasp that immortality for the dead is appointed at a specific time. The dead wake up at the *Last Trumpet* to receive their gift of immortality. It does NOT happen the minute someone dies.

Many funerals that I have attended have preachers who speak of the deceased as being in heaven, looking down on everyone. According to Scripture, this is not true. We are waiting for the resurrection to happen first:

"So will it be with the resurrection of the dead. The body that is sown is perishable; it is raised imperishable; it is sown in dishonor; it is raised in glory; it is sown in weakness; it is raised in power; it is sown a natural body and raised a spiritual body. If there is a natural body, there is also a spiritual body."

(1 Corinthians 15:42-44)

Until the Resurrection, the dead are *"mortal"* and *"corruptible."* But when that great Trumpet sounds, the sleeping saints will awaken: *"raised in incorruption," "raised in power,"* and *"raised with a spiritual body."* These precious souls will rise from their graves, gifted with immortality forevermore.

The Prophet Daniel foretold a day when *"many of those who sleep in the dust of the earth shall awake" (Daniel 12:2)*. Those who have rested in dark caskets will awaken to one of two resurrections. They will rise from their slumber, realizing that their reward has arrived. Those who have done evil will wake to *'everlasting shame"* and face *"everlasting destruction,"* not everlasting *destroying. (2 Thessalonians 1:9)*

Daniel's prophecy does not suggest that the dead and wicked are alive in a fiery torture chamber. Instead, he indicates that they will one day awaken from the *"dust of the earth,"* not from a burning pit. The dead are in a state of sleep, awaiting resurrection, rather than down in the depths of the earth, screaming, cursing, and being taunted by demons of terror.

Even Daniel wrote about his resurrection. He was told, *"You will rest, and stand in your lot at the end of days" (Daniel 12:13).* The term "rest" is often associated with death. For example, Revelation states,

"Blessed are the dead who die in the Lord from now on. "Yes," says the Spirit, "that they may rest from their labors..."

(Revelation 14:13)

Rest symbolizes the peace of a sound sleep. Daniel is blessed and currently in a deep sleep, and one day, he will awaken at the *"end of days,"* fully rested and joyfully standing above the grave from which he was raised.

Job anticipated the day of God's Indignation and wished he could hide in the grave until God's Wrath had passed. He understood that his Creator had set an appointed time when his Redeemer would remember him as he lay in the dust of the earth. This faithful believer was unafraid of death's temporary hold.

Job asked, *"If a man dies, shall he live again?"* Confidently answering his question, he said, *"All the days of my appointed time will I wait until my change comes. You shall call, and I will answer You." (Job 14:13-15)*

Job clearly understood his fate at the end of his life. He stated, *"I will lie down in the dust, and you will seek me, but I will be no more" (Job 7:21).* The phrase "ashes to ashes, dust to dust" is derived from Scripture, as seen in this passage.

This great and faithful servant of God understood that humanity would *"die and waste away"* and *"give up the spirit."* He pondered, *"Where is he?"* Concluding:

"So man lies down and does not rise; until the heavens are no more, they will not awake, nor be roused from their sleep." (Job 14:10, 12)

Job's perspective on death reflects a profound acceptance of the human condition and the natural cycle of life and death. His words convey a sense of resignation to the inevitability of mortality. But the promise is sure. Yeshua declared:

"I am the Resurrection and the Life. He who believes in Me, though he may die, he shall live." (John 11:25)

Those who sleep are not aware of their surroundings. They don't communicate or disturb anyone else (except the snorers!). Most sleepers have their eyes closed, and those who sleep with their eyes open cannot see beyond the darkness. Sleepers do not move around much. Similarly, the sleep of death restrains life's ambitions and emotions. No getting up or down, no yelling or screeching, no damned souls roaring as they grind their teeth in anger—just silence.

Unlike the concept of Hell, one day the wicked will *"sleep a perpetual sleep and not wake up" (Jeremiah 51:57).* It seems evil will eventually lie down and be put to death, never to wake again.

Death's Inactivity

Solomon, one of the wisest men ever, received direct revelation about what happens at death. He shares:

"The dead know nothing... also their love, their hatred, and their envy has now perished"... "There is no knowledge, or wisdom in the grave where you are going."

(Ecclesiastes 9:5-6)

According to this declaration, not much happens after a man dies. The dead do not know or feel anything. Death holds no knowledge of hatred, nor can one in the grave be tempted to hate. How can there be a "Hell" where hatred rules - if hatred perishes at death? King Solomon refutes that anyone can hate or feel anything in the grave.

Because of this profound truth, Solomon urges us with this advice:

"Whatever your hand finds to do, do it with your might; for there is no work or device or knowledge or wisdom in the grave where you are going." (Ecclesiastes 9:10)

Since no activity is happening below the ground, making the most of our time and efforts while we are alive is essential. Recognizing that our earthly lives are finite, we should approach our tasks with dedication and zeal. Knowing that there is no opportunity for work, knowledge, or wisdom in the grave should inspire us to act with purpose and passion in the present.

HELL'S PROPHECY

King David clearly stated, *"The dead do not praise the Lord, neither any that go down to silence" (Psalm 117:15).* Whatever happens below is relatively silent. The dead do not ascend at death—they descend. Hollering and screaming in the hot sulfur baths of Hades cannot be accurate. There is *silence when the dead arrive underground.*

As we have learned, many believers assume that when a person dies, they go straight to their reward, whether they are saved or a sinner. Scholars often cite the conversation between Jesus and the thief on the cross to support their notion that people immediately reach their eternal destiny upon death. So, let's ponder this narrative.

As the thief hung there on a cross next to the Savior of the world, just before he died, it became evident to this bandit that Yeshua was the Son of God. The thief acknowledged:

"Do you not even fear God since you are under the same judgment? We are punished justly, for we are receiving what our actions deserve. But this man has done nothing wrong. Lord, remember me when you come into your Kingdom." (Luke 23:40-42)

In response, Jesus replied, *"Assuredly, I say to you, today you will be with Me in Paradise." (Luke 23:43)*

On the surface, Jesus told the thief they would meet in Paradise on the day of their death. However, a thorough examination of the entire testimony reveals that Jesus did not meet the thief in Paradise that same day.

Remember, the original Greek translation did not include commas in the rendering of this text. Later, the translators placed a comma where it seemed to imply Jesus would meet the thief on that very day. However, by examining other evidence provided by John, we will discover that Jesus' soul was in the grave for three days.

Oh, what a picture of grace and divine intent. The God of Mercy revealed His True Nature to a thief who had mocked Him. Just before this criminal died, he came face to face with the Truth. Often, it takes the prospect of death for people to realize that eternity is just ahead.

In this grand illustration of sacrifice, the Hand of Love extended an open invitation, welcoming the thief into Paradise in his final moments. Jesus didn't threaten him with eternal torment—He offered the bandit Paradise.

When Yeshua died, He entrusted His Spirit to His Father with His final breath. This historical moment testifies that as He was dying in His final moments:

"Jesus cried out with a loud voice" and proclaimed, *"Father, into Your Hands I commit my Spirit."...having said this, He breathed His last" (Luke 23:46).* Jesus died, His Spirit left Him, and He remained dead for three days.

Solomon explains what happens at death this way:

"Then shall the dust return to the Earth as it was, and the Spirit shall return to God who gave it" (Ecclesiastes 12:7).

Just as the Spirit returned to the Father when Jesus died, it is with all who die. The Bible illustrates that a person's soul dies when the breath is removed from the body and returns to the dust from which it came.

King David described the dying process: *"His breath goes forth; he returns to his Earth; in that very day his thoughts perish"* (Psalm 146:4). This indicates that the soul's mind ceases; even thoughts vanish. Once the breath leaves, the dead cannot communicate with anyone, as the mind can no longer generate thoughts. If people recognized this Biblical truth, they would not mess with modern-day mediums or chase after ghosts.

The prophecy foretold Yeshua's Resurrection, revealing that Jesus' soul would be in the grave, not in the Father's presence at His Death:

"Jesus... whom God raised up, having loosed the pains of death because it is not possible that He should be held by it"; and he adds, *"for you will not leave My Soul in Hades" (Acts 2:24, 22).* His Spirit left Him and returned to the Father, while His soul entered the grave (Hades).

John testified that after Yeshua had been in the tomb for three days and had risen from the dead, He found Mary at the tomb. When Mary went to touch the Risen Savior, He cautioned her:

"Do not cling to me, for I have not yet ascended to My Father" (John 20:16-17).

Did the thief go to heaven with Yeshua on the day they both died? No, the thief did not go to Paradise that very same day. Even after three days, Yeshua had not yet ascended to His Father's Presence. Could He have met the thief on the day of His Death? No way.

Did Jesus lie to the thief or mislead Mary? Neither - He was truthful with both. The Savior had not yet been to Paradise. After His Resurrection, He told Mary:

"I am ascending to My Father" (John 20:17).

The grave could no longer hold Him, and He was ready to see His Father. Yeshua ascended into Paradise three days after His Death, but not on the same day, He spoke to the thief.

Death's Inactivity

While hanging on the cross, the thief was promised to meet Yeshua in Paradise, where God dwells. According to the Bible, Jesus will raise the thief on *"the Last Day"*:

"And this is the Will of Him who sent Me, that I shall lose none of all those He has given Me, but raise them up at the Last Day." (John 6:39)

At that time, the resurrected thief will *"eat from the Tree of Life, which is in the midst of the Paradise of God," alongside Jesus (Revelation 2:7). Paradise is the dwelling place of Yahweh and Yeshua*. This place awaits those who overcome.

If these clear revelations are not enough to convince a seeker of truth who doubts the soul's finality of death, consider this vivid picture of death's dominion:

"They that trust in their wealth and boast in the multitude of their riches, none can by any means redeem his brother, nor give God a ransom for him; for the redemption of their soul is costly and ceases forever; that he should still live forever and not see corruption. He sees that wise men die. Likewise, the fool and the senseless person perish and leave their wealth to others." (Psalm 49:6-10)

All the money in the world is just a "drop in the bucket" compared to the actual cost of a soul's redemption. According to this revelation, the souls of those who trusted in their possessions will ultimately *"cease forever."* The Bible clarifies that the senseless person who places their faith in riches will *"die"* and *"perish."*

True salvation and eternal life cannot be bought but are gifts that come through faith and grace in Yeshua, the Messiah. Trusting in riches leads to a dead end, literally and spiritually, as wealth cannot prevent the inevitability of death or secure a place beyond it. Contrary to popular opinion:

"The soul who sins will die." (Ezekiel 18:4)

Yeshua warns us that the ungodly soul will ultimately face extinction. He advised people not to fear those who could only kill the body but not touch the soul. Instead, He urged them to heed a more significant warning:

*"Fear Him who is able to **destroy** both body and soul in Gehenna" (Matthew 10:28).*

This powerful statement serves as a distinct caution to all, recognizing that Yeshua alone holds the Authority to *"destroy both body and soul"* in the eternal fire of Judgment.

When the Hell?

Jesus declared, "Do not marvel at this; the hour is coming when all who are in their graves will hear His voice and come forth —those who have done good to the Resurrection of Life, and those who have done evil to the Resurrection of Condemnation."

— (John 5:28)

Whatever one believes about a literal burning Hell happening "underneath - down yonder" must be tested against Scripture. Numerous Scriptures indicate a Resurrection of both believers in Jesus and for the unbelievers.

For those who have done good, there is the "*Resurrection of Life,*" and for those who have done evil, there is the "*Resurrection of Condemnation*" *(John 5:28-29).* Therefore, any concept of going to Hell will have to wait until then.

Based on this truth, a wicked person waits in their grave until they hear the voice of Jesus. Then, they will rise from the grave to be condemned. In this Resurrection, the Judge will make the sorrowful pronouncement, "*I don't know you,*" and *then* the execution will commence.

Make no mistake, no rewards or punishments in Hell will occur until the Lord of Lords returns to give each one what they deserve, not before then:

"*For the Son of Man will come in the Glory of His Father with His Angels, and then He will reward each according to his works.*"

(Matthew 16:27)

HELL'S PROPHECY

It is clear from Jesus' teachings that there is no *"pit of Hell"* in the center of the Earth where millions are in excruciating agony, and the devils are striking little children continually with hot iron pitchforks after they die.

Prophetic scenarios suggest that unsaved individuals are dead in their graves, awaiting a decision from the Judge's Chambers; after all the evidence has been examined and guilt is determined, the Judge's pronouncement will then be made.

Consider an analogy: Imagine someone accused of murder being sentenced to prison before the evidence is even heard. Our legal system requires a trial before someone is imprisoned. Similarly, Yahweh's Justice operates on the same principle. The wicked dead are kept in their graves, akin to a jailhouse, awaiting their punishment. Justice is only met after they are judged and found guilty. Guilt must be established before sentencing.

We have discovered that a fundamental principle of fairness and due process reflects the Divine justice that mirrors human legal systems. The courts mandate a just and fair trial before imposing a sentence. Contrary to popular opinion, Hell is not in operation. It is "out of order."

It is imperative to recognize the timing of the execution of the death sentence. Peter offers a clear insight regarding the Day of Reckoning, stating:

"The Lord knows how to reserve the unjust under punishment for the Day of Judgment" (2 Peter 2:9).

This aligns with the Bible's apparent stance that the punishment of the unjust is *reserved* (put on hold) until the Day of Judgment, a future event. How can someone visit Hell when there is no such place?

When the Hell?

There is no fiery hole yet – *"the present Heavens and Earth are reserved for fire, being kept for the Day of Judgment and the destruction of the ungodly." (2 Peter 3:7)*

The Scriptures teach that once a person dies, they wait in the jailhouse "reserved" and "kept" until they see the Judge to be destroyed.

"Just as people are destined to die once, and after that to face Judgment." (Hebrews 9:27)

Until that time, the unsaved remain in their graves, awaiting their sentencing and the subsequent enactment of justice. Hell will have no fury until then.

There is no Hell until Judgment Day. When Jesus returns, He will:

"Judge the living and the dead at His Appearing and His Kingdom." (2 Timothy 4:1).

The final Judgment and the resurrection are put on hold as ultimate Justice is deferred until Judgment Day.

Yeshua will come *"with ten thousand of His saints to execute Judgment upon all, and to convict all the ungodly among them of all their ungodly deeds which they have done in an ungodly way." (Jude 1:14-15)*

This will be a shocking appearance! The conviction will be final when Yeshua appears—a done deal. The decree will be,

He who is unjust, let him be unjust still; he who is filthy, let him be filthy still; he who is righteous, let him be righteous still; he who is holy, let him be holy still." (Revelation 22:11). It will be too late to change it after death. A great gulf has been fixed.

HELL'S PROPHECY

There are no indications in the Bible that the wicked are burning in Hell before their resurrection. It is a complete fallacy to believe otherwise. Is the fallacy of Hell becoming clearer yet?

Where the Hell?

Therefore, I will make the heavens tremble, and the Earth will be shaken from its place at the Wrath of the Lord of Hosts on the Day of His Burning Anger.

— *(Isaiah 13:13)*

The Earth will undergo a two-phase destruction process to purge it of evil. Just before Yeshua returns, the planet will experience Birth Pangs. Fire will play a significant role in eradicating the wicked, first at Yeshua's Return and then at the resurrection of evil.

The Earth will be in a catastrophic state as the world's Savior returns to gather His Faithful. Just before His Arrival, the Bowls of His Wrath will be poured out in Judgment on a world gone mad. Whether we want to accept it or not, we are reminded that a massive flood of water once destroyed the world.

Remember, a flood destroyed the World once before because Yahweh *"was sorry that He had made man on the Earth, and He was grieved in His Heart."* He determined:

"I am going to put an end to all people, for the Earth is filled with violence because of them. I am surely going to destroy both them and the Earth". God observed the profound corruption of the Earth, as all its inhabitants had deviated from their righteous ways." (Genesis 6:11-13)

Based on the prophetic evidence, the people of the Earth will again become so rebellious because:

HELL'S PROPHECY

"The wickedness of man was great on the Earth, and every imagination of the thoughts of his heart was only evil continually" (Genesis 6:5).

The first time, Yahweh used water to obliterate humanity due to their evil. Now, the next time Judgment falls, Fire will descend upon the Earth, bringing its ultimate destruction. All wicked individuals will be destroyed, just as they were the first time, not by water but by Fire.

The Bible prophesies that in the last days, the Earth's inhabitants will once more replicate the evil deeds that led to previous destruction. One Biblical writer makes this plain:

"But mark this: There will be terrible times in the Last Days. People will be lovers of themselves, lovers of money, boastful, proud, abusive, disobedient to their parents, ungrateful, unholy, without love, unforgiving, slanderous, without self-control, brutal, not lovers of the good, treacherous, rash, conceited, lovers of pleasure rather than lovers of God—having a form of godliness but denying its power." (2 Timothy 3:1-4)

It is on this Earth that Judgment by fire will begin. For the rebellious, Yeshua will repay them for creating a chaotic world, thus invoking His Wrath upon them. This is His Act of Vengeance.

Those of us who are alive when He returns will witness that:

"It is a righteous thing with God to repay with tribulation those who trouble you, and to you who are troubled rest with us, when the Lord Yeshua shall be revealed from Heaven with His Mighty Angels, in flaming fire taking vengeance on those who do not know God, and on those who do not obey the gospel of our Lord Jesus Christ. "These people will face the penalty of eternal destruction, separated from the Presence of the Lord and the Glory of His Power." (2 Thessalonians 1:7-9)

Where the Hell?

The Almighty's Fire will descend upon the wicked, and they will incur the penalty of *eternal destruction*, not eternal destruction. The fire from Yeshua will annihilate them, and its effect will be everlasting. There is a distinction between destruction (finality) and destroying (continual). Another Prophet prophesied of this exact time:

"See, Yahweh Comes with Fire, and His Chariots are like a whirlwind; He will unleash His Wrath with fury and His Rebuke with flames of fire. For Yahweh will Execute Judgment by fire and by His Sword upon humanity, and many will be those slain by Yahweh." (Isaiah 66:15-16)

The Almighty established a way for people to love and bless one another. However, they rejected His Son's offer and followed their evil hearts. Because of this, Yahweh's Anger showers the disobedient with fire that slays them. Historically, to be slain means to be lifeless, and God's Execution is frequently compared to killing in Scripture.

What a fearful day of reckoning it will be for those who are willfully ignorant. Some argue that the fire and Yahweh's furious anger are not harsh enough punishments. Are you kidding me? What kind of spirit do these complainers possess? Picture this:

"The Day of the Lord will come as a thief in the night; in which the elements shall melt with fervent heat, the Earth also, and the works therein shall be burned up" (2 Peter 3:10).

How can anyone misinterpret *"burned up"*? Will not God's Fire bring absolute cremation? This portrayal of our Savior's intent is not one of eternal torment but of the complete and utter end of all torment.

HELL'S PROPHECY

The Prophet Zephaniah declared that fire would consume the earth, devouring everything. There is no hint of a pit at the center of the Earth where souls are being tortured:

"Neither their silver nor their gold will be able to deliver them on the Day of Yahweh's Wrath. The whole Earth will be consumed by the Fire of His Jealousy." Indeed, He will make a sudden end of all who dwell on the Earth." (Zephaniah 1:18)

"Devoured" means *consumed, eaten up, destroyed*, or *wasted*. When the Day of God's Anger arrives, the fire will conclude the lives of everyone *on Earth*. The whole land will be left in desolation. This proclamation does not hint at a fiery, screaming underworld, just a *"sudden end,"* indicating that it will not take an eternity to accomplish His Purpose.

"I will completely sweep away everything from the face of the Earth," declares Yahweh. *"I will sweep away man and beast; I will sweep away the birds of the air, the fish of the sea, and the idols with their wicked worshipers. I will cut off humankind from the face of the Earth,"* declares Yahweh. *(Zephaniah 1:2-3)*

This powerful declaration by Yahweh is a profound warning of Impending Judgment. Not only humans but all living creatures—beasts, birds, and fish—are included in this sweeping Judgment. The descriptive language of sweeping away everything *"from the face of the Earth"* implies a complete and irreversible final answer to evil without leaving a trace of it. How about this picture:

"For behold, the Day is coming, burning like an oven, and all the proud, yes, all who do wickedly, will be stubble. And the Day which is coming shall burn them up," Says Yahweh of Hosts, "That will leave them neither root nor branch...You shall trample the

Where the Hell?

wicked, for they shall be ashes under the soles of your feet on the day that I do this," Says Yahweh of Hosts." (Malachi 4:1,3)

How can anyone see a *"hell hole"* in this revelation of a Consuming Fire? The Earth will burn like a hot oven, where the wicked will be turned into *"stubble"* with *"no root"* and *"no branch."* In Hebrew, the root symbolizes origin and foundation, with the branch representing growth and the future. The complete burning up of both indicates the complete eradication of the wicked, leaving no possibility for it to exist anymore. According to the Prophet Malachi, the wicked will be *ashes* under our feet someday.

Consider the end of the wicked in this light:

"Behold, the Day of The Lord comes Cruel, with both Wrath and Fierce Anger, to lay the land desolate; and He will Destroy its sinners from it." (Isaiah 13:9)

Again, there is no proof that the wicked will live on forever. Death, destruction, and desolation will be the results of rebellion against the Creator. The fire will burn everything into absolute ashes and desolation on Earth. Who will be able to survive Yahweh's Wrath? Does this sound like anything but absolute ruination?

The Bible is clear about where the destruction of the wicked takes place. The activity of Yahweh's destruction occurs on this Earth, on the ground itself. This presents a vivid picture of total desolation, with no trace of demons or devils with pitchforks running around tormenting the gnashers of teeth.

"On the wicked, He will rain fiery coals and burning sulfur; a scorching wind will be their lot." (Psalm 11:6)

The fire that devours will come from above in the heavens, not from the Earth's center. It is on the Earth's surface where this consuming fire will occur, not from its core. It is vital to recognize where evildoers receive their Judgment: out of the ground, not beneath it. The condemned are not descending to *Hell* to receive their reward; they are rising from the grave to face the Judge's judgment.

The author of the book "*23 Minutes in Hell*" claims to know, having taken a trip to Hell, that it is:

"*thirty-seven hundred miles deep... Hell does exist. It is in the center of the Earth.*"[26]

Nowhere in all the testimonies of God's Word has there been any attestation that supports the idea of Hell being 3,700 miles deep within the Earth's center. On the contrary:

"For behold, Yahweh comes forth from His Dwelling Place; He will Come Down and tread on the high places of the Earth. The mountains will melt beneath Him, and the valleys will split apart, like wax before the fire, like water rushing down a slope." (Micah 1:3-4)

By now, it becomes increasingly evident that the fallacy of Hell is a massive stretch of the imagination with an extreme lack of Biblical support. The popular image of a torture chamber in the center of the Earth is not supported by any Scriptural evidence. The Prophecies depict a distinct fire coming from Yeshua in the first order of destroying the wicked who are alive when He returns to Earth:

"The Earth trembled and quaked, and the foundations of the mountains shook; they trembled because He was Angry. Smoke rose from His Nostrils; Consuming Fire came from His Mouth, and burning coals blazed out of it." (Psalm 18:7-8)

How can anyone imagine living through the Devouring Fire of God's Mouth? Imagine the Earth-shaking, mountains quaking, and the Devouring Fire all coming from the overwhelming and devastating impact of His Anger. Can you imagine anyone surviving through the Devouring Fire of God's Mouth? Yahweh will *devour* all that is unholy. His power will consume and destroy evil - period.

"Yahweh will roar from on high; He will thunder from His Holy Dwelling and Roar mightily against His Land. He will shout like those who tread the grapes against all who live on Earth. The tumult will resound to the ends of the Earth, for Yahweh will bring charges against the nations; He will bring Judgment on all mankind and put the wicked to the sword."

"On that Day, a great whirlwind will rise from the farthest parts of the Earth. The slain of Yahweh will stretch from one end of the Earth to the other. They will not be mourned, gathered, or buried; they will be left on the ground" (Jeremiah 25:30-33).

According to the prophet, the slain of the Lord will cover the Earth from one end to the other. When someone is slain, they are lifeless. This prophetic image clearly shows that the many who are killed will lie scattered on the surface of the Earth. No cries, pitchforks, or two-horned, red-tailed devils will taunt or torment anyone in this depiction of the end. When Yahweh wields His Sword against evil, it will bring complete and final destruction to those cut down by it.

Picture the devastation and condition of a world that rejected the offer of Yahweh's Son. Now, a great gulf is fixed between believer and unbeliever:

"Yahweh is going to lay waste the Earth and devastate it; He will ruin its face and scatter its inhabitants—The Earth will be entirely laid waste and totally plundered. Yahweh has spoken this

Word. The Earth dries up and withers, the world languishes and withers, the heavens languish with the Earth.

The Earth is defiled by its people; they have disobeyed the laws, violated the statutes, and broken the everlasting covenant. Therefore, a curse consumes the Earth; its people must bear their guilt. Therefore, Earth's inhabitants are burned up, and very few are left". (Isaiah 24:1,3-6)

Imagine how horrendous the Earth's obliteration is because of the rebellion of humanity against their Maker. We should be careful not to trivialize Yahweh's Law and Covenants made for us. We are warned that disobeying Him will result in absolute destruction and annihilation. The wicked are *consumed, and the few who survive are those who have remained* faithful to the end. They have gone to their reward of eternal life.

Another Prophet saw this same horror-filled devastation and prophesied:

"I looked at the Earth, and it was formless and empty, and at the heavens, their light was gone. I looked at the mountains, which were quaking; all the hills were swaying. I looked, and there were no people; every bird in the sky had flown away. (Jeremiah 4:23-25)

What a picture of absolute extinction. The Earth is dark, desolate, and devoid of life. However, the prophecy declares this is not the total end yet:

"Fear, and the pit, and the snare, are upon thee, O inhabitant of the Earth. And it shall come to pass, that he who flees from the noise of the fear shall fall into the pit; and he that comes up out of the midst of the pit shall be taken in the snare: for the windows from on high are open, and the foundations of the Earth will shake.

The Earth is broken up; the Earth is split asunder, and the Earth is violently shaken. The Earth reels like a drunkard; it sways like a hut in the wind; so heavy upon it is the guilt of its rebellion that it falls—never to rise again.

"On that day, Yahweh will punish the powers in the heavens above and the Kings on the Earth below. They will be herded together like prisoners bound in a dungeon; they will be shut up in prison and punished after many days." (Isaiah 24:17-23)

Imagine a desolate world, the Earth utterly broken, with death and everlasting destruction at every corner of what was once the perfect Grand Design. As if the great shaking caused by man's transgression was not enough, the Almighty will revisit them. They have died once, but after a thousand years, they will emerge from the prison house one last time for Judgment. After many days, they will face the Courtroom for sentencing once again.

"The nations raged, the kingdoms were moved; He uttered His Voice, the Earth melted" (Psalm 46:6).

The notion of an eternal torture chamber called "Hell" becomes increasingly questionable as evidence mounts against it. This narrative shows that the unjust will perish on the Earth's surface, not beneath it. The image of the entire Earth melting and quaking with *"no man left"* alive stands in stark contrast to the belief in eternal conscious torment.

"Therefore, since all these things will be dissolved, what kind of people ought you to be in holy conduct and godliness, looking for and hastening the coming of the Day of Yahweh, because of which the Heavens will be dissolved, being on fire, and the elements will melt with fervent heat." (2 Peter 3:11-12)

So, how should we respond to Peter's question? Knowing these events are imminent, how should we live our lives in holiness, striving to please the One who has the power to save or destroy us soon? Are we looking forward to and asking for the day when Yeshua returns to save us from this crooked and perverse generation?

We have discovered that "Hell" (The Earth) will be *burned up, melted, a*nd *dissolved.* Myths and legends have shaped what we have heard or understood about Hell. The Bible is clear. Where is "Hell"? We are standing on it. One day, it will be covered in a Lake of Fire.

Why the Hell?

"For we know Him who said, 'It is Mine to Avenge; I Will Repay,' and again, 'The Lord will Judge His People.' It is dreadful to fall into the Hands of the Living God."

— *(Hebrews 10:30-31)*

Throughout history, the vulnerable and less fortunate have consistently faced hardship. From the financial elite, unjust rulers of nations, con artists, bullies, and the self-centered, to all others who suppress and oppress the poor, these individuals have often wielded their power and influence ruthlessly, disregarding the harm they inflict on others.

The Almighty Yahweh will open the books that have recorded the evil deeds of the wicked folks and will sit in Judgment, repaying them for the wrongs they have committed. Yes, there will be a payday for those who do evil.

The Apostle James illustrates this injustice with this narrative:

"Now listen, you rich people, weep and wail because of the misery that is coming upon you. Your wealth has rotted, and moths have eaten your clothes. Your gold and silver are corroded; their corrosion will testify against you and consume your flesh like fire. You have hoarded wealth in these last days.

Look! The wages you failed to pay the workers who mowed your fields are crying out against you. The cries of the harvesters have reached the ears of the Lord Almighty. You have lived on Earth in luxury and self-indulgence. You have fattened yourselves for the Day of Slaughter. You have condemned and murdered the innocent one who was not opposing you." (James 5:1-6)

This passage vividly portrays greed and criminal intent. The obsession with money and wealth has led many to sell their souls to the devil. A system of slavery has emerged through debt. Credit card companies and banks lure people in, only to enslave them under their bondage. Adding to this are the courts that legislate unjust laws to strip people of everything they own. Crooked lawyers, devoid of compassion, exploit the vulnerable for profit. Yet, one day, the tide will turn.

Yahweh Himself will avenge all wrongdoing against the vulnerable. No evil act will go unnoticed. There will be a time of accountability when Justice will be served. This should inspire us to live lives of integrity, compassion, and empathy, knowing that our actions have eternal significance and will be judged by the Highest Authority.

Those who have willfully mocked God and ignored *"the Work of Yahweh, neither considered the Operation of His Hands" (Isaiah 5:12)* have chosen their fate. Why would Yahweh want to keep someone around who hates and denies Him?

Consider this:

"How much more severely do you think someone deserves to be punished who has trampled the Son of God underfoot, who has treated as an unholy thing the Blood of the Covenant that sanctified them, and who has insulted the Spirit of Grace? (Hebrews 10:29)

The person who hears and dismisses the gospel as a fable insults the Eternal Life-Giver. What Yahweh sent to save us through His Beloved Son cannot save the unbeliever who rejects it. They fail to consider the suffering the Father endured,

Why the Hell?

watching His Only Son tortured unjustly. God's accomplished Work, immense Sacrifice, and boundless Love have all been denied and rejected. For this reason, Yahweh pronounces:

"I will make justice the measuring line and righteousness the level. Hail will sweep away your refuge of lies, and water will flood your hiding place." (Isaiah 28:17)

Yahweh has a standard or measure of righteousness akin to a plumb line used in construction to ensure structures are faithful and upright. There will be a forceful and decisive eradication of falsehoods and deceit. Hail, with its destructive power, symbolizes the cleansing effect that leaves no place for lies to hide. God will bring an overwhelming flood that exposes and washes away anything wicked, hidden, or concealed. Those who have trusted in the lies spread throughout the Earth will find no sanctuary. The vicious towards humanity will be held accountable:

"People shall be brought down, each man shall be humbled, and the eyes of the lofty shall be humbled. But Yahweh of Hosts shall be exalted in Judgment, and Yahweh who is Holy shall be hallowed in righteousness. Therefore, Sheol has enlarged itself and opened its mouth beyond measure; Their glory, multitude, and pomp, and he who is jubilant shall descend into it."

(Isaiah 5:15-16,14)

The self-centered who live in vanity and oppress others will face their fate. Those mean-spirited individuals who disregard the value of respecting God's Creation will be judged unworthy of eternal life. Pure terror and the ultimate humbling of the proud and arrogant will bring them to their knees. Human glory and pomp are fleeting. Proper exaltation belongs to the King of Kings and Lord of Lords, who will be revered in righteousness.

HELL'S PROPHECY

The picture of *Sheol*, the realm of the dead, *"enlarging itself"* and opening *"its mouth without measure,"* illuminates the downfall of those who have acted unjustly and arrogantly. The consequences of living a life devoid of respect for God's Creation and moral principles will be beyond frightening:

"Woe to those who decree unrighteous laws and write misfortune they have prescribed, who turn aside the needy from justice, and take away the right from the poor of My People, making widows their prey, and robbing the fatherless. What will you do on the Day of Visitation, in the desolation from afar? To whom will you flee for help, and where will you leave your glory?" (Isaiah 5:2-3)

The Almighty Yahweh will visit the unjust leaders and corrupt systems that exploit the vulnerable. As those in power, they had a moral and ethical responsibility to uphold justice and protect the rights of the needy, the poor, widows, and orphans. Yes, there will be a *"Day of Visitation,"* when God will bring justice and hold the unjust accountable for their actions. In the face of Divine Disgust, there will be nowhere to hide or seek help.

It is now too late to recognize that true religion was *"to visit the fatherless and widows in their affliction" (James 1:27).* True religion involves caring for society's most vulnerable, specifically the fatherless and widows. Genuine faith is demonstrated through compassionate actions and serving others rather than through rituals or passive beliefs.

"For the extortioner will come to an end, the spoiler will cease, and the oppressors will be consumed from the land" (Isaiah 16:4). *"For it is a people of no understanding; therefore, He who made them will have no mercy on them, and He who formed them will show them no favor"* (Isaiah 27:11).

Why the Hell?

The bad of society must be held accountable. The Scriptures warn against the oppressor, ignorant and merciless. There will be an end to those who exploit and oppress others. The people's lack of understanding and willful ignorance will lead to a withdrawal of Yahweh's Divine Mercy and Favor.

"It will be a Spirit of Judgment for the one who sits in judgment" (Isaiah 28:6). *"For He will have Judgment without mercy for those who have shown no mercy because mercy triumphs over Judgment" (James 2:13).*

Even in His Mercy, He will Judge the unforgiving. Thank God, Mercy will balance His Judgment. He also expects us to be merciful. Mercy supersedes Judgment. If we have not shown mercy as we have received from Him, there will be none for us.

Why the "Hell"? There will be payback to the demonic forces who have gone after the Followers of Yeshua for two millennia. The Bible notes those followers who:

"Were tortured, refusing to be released so that they might gain an even better Resurrection. Some faced jeers and flogging, and even chains and imprisonment. They were put to death by stoning; they were sawed in two; the sword killed them. They went about in sheepskins and goatskins, destitute, persecuted, and mistreated— the world was not worthy of them. They wandered in deserts and mountains, living in caves and holes in the ground." (Hebrews 11:35-38)

Millions of followers who have dedicated their lives to the cause of the Savior have stood up in the face of tremendous satanic opposition from God Haters all over the world. Even within the ranks of God Chasers came deep persecution, who executed millions in Yeshua's Name. But, let it be known, The One who *"Created all things"* promised His Adopted:

"Do not fear any of those things you are about to suffer. Indeed, the devil is about to throw some of you into prison, that you may be tested, and you will have tribulation... Be faithful until death, and I will give you the Crown of Life." (Revelation 2:10)

When the Seals are stripped from the scroll of Judgments just before Yeshua's return to pay back those who brought tribulation to His Children, He reassures the Martyred that one day He will take care of business and reward His Faithful, already honored. John the Revelator shares the vision:

"When He opened the fifth seal, I saw under the altar the souls of those who had been slain because of the Word of God and the testimony they had maintained. They loudly said, "How long, Sovereign Lord, Holy, and True, until You Judge the Earth's inhabitants and avenge our blood?"

Then, a white robe was given to each of them. And they were told to rest a little longer until the full number of their brothers and sisters—their fellow servants of Jesus who were to be martyred—had joined them." (Revelation 6:9-11)

Year after year, decade after decade, the One who shed His Blood to save those who would believe watched with great agony the saints who had shed their blood for Him. Yes - until Yeshua Returns, more will give up their lives, but it will not go unnoticed as it is written:

"Your Hand will lay hold on all your enemies; Your Right Hand will seize your foes. When You appear for battle, You will burn them up as in a blazing furnace. Yahweh will swallow them up in His Wrath, and His Fire will consume them." (Psalm 21:8-9)

This is a vivid picture of Yahweh's Anger, swallowing up and devouring those who hate Him. There's not much left when a person devours a good T-bone steak! Similarly, nothing will be left of the wicked after God ingests them. Count on it; the Fire of His Anger will ultimately consume the wicked.

Because of His Great Mercy, God will remove the rabid dogs and put them out of their misery. It would be a literal "Hell" for the Rebellious towards humanity to live in a world of absolute peace and harmony, where love and righteousness rule.

Considering these things, let us heed this warning:

"Do not be deceived; God is not mocked; for whatever a man sows, he will reap. For the one who sows to his flesh will reap destruction from the flesh, but the one who sows to the Spirit will reap eternal life from the Spirit." (Galatians 6:7-8)

Why the Hell?

For too long, the innocent have tolerated evil people. Eternal Bliss can only come when Our Defender rids the world of schemers, scammers, scandalous scumbags, scoundrels, Scallywags, scurrilous scofflaws, and scrooges. For those who choose to go their own way, disregarding humanity and the Creator, they will be held accountable.

The First Resurrection

"For My Father's Will is that everyone who looks to the Son and believes in Him shall have eternal life, and I will raise them up at the Last Day."

— (John 6:40)

The Bible foretells a profound event of great reward from the Father's Hand, known as the "First Resurrection":

"Blessed are those who have part in the First Resurrection, upon which the Second Death has no power." (Revelation 20:6)

On this extraordinary day, all faithful believers who walk the narrow path of the Father's Way will receive the promised rewards from Yahweh's bountiful Treasure House. The faithful who died holding onto the hope of a future resurrection will hear the voice of Yeshua calling them from their graves, rising triumphantly over death. He who has the *"keys to Hell and Death"* will lead them into eternal life. It is written:

"The Lord will descend from Heaven with a powerful command. Accompanied by the voice of the Archangel and the Trumpet Call of God, the dead in Yeshua will rise first." (1 Thes 4:16-17)

The victory over death and fulfilling God's promises are now revealed. Having remained steadfast in their beliefs, the faithful are honored with a miraculous Resurrection and rewarded for their unwavering faith and commitment. They rise in victory from the grave into eternal life.

The First Resurrection

What a majestic rescue this is. Jesus promised that one day, He would return to Earth. He comforted those who heard Him with these words of honor and assurance:

"Do not let your hearts be troubled. You believe in God; believe in Me as well. In My Father's house are many mansions. If it were not so, would I have told you that I am going there to prepare a place for you? And if I go and prepare a place for you, I will come again and receive you to Myself; that where I am, there you may be also." (John 14:1-3)

At the appointed time of Earth's Closure, Yeshua comes back as:

"The sign of the Son of Man will appear in heaven, and then all the tribes of the Earth will mourn, and they will see the Son of Man Coming on the clouds of heaven with Power and Great Glory. And He will send His Angels with a great sound of a Trumpet, and they will gather together His Elect from the four winds, from one end of heaven to the other." (Matthew 24:30-31)

The Prophet Isaiah spoke of this fantastic and glorious day centuries before it occurred. He boldly proclaimed the future resurrection:

"Your dead will live, Yahweh; their bodies will rise—let those who dwell in the dust wake up and shout for joy—your dew is like the dew of the morning; the Earth will give birth to her dead."

Jesus will call out to His children with a powerful command:

"Awake and sing, you who dwell in the dust." (Isaiah 26:19)

As if awakened from a deep slumber, the faithful believers arise, transformed *"in a flash, in the twinkling of an eye, at the Last Trumpet" (1 Corinthians 15:51)*. When the Trumpet sounds, those bound by mortality are resurrected to immortal life. The corruptible will become incorruptible, and the mortal will embrace immortality as they stand before the Almighty King of Kings.

The sound of God's Seventh Trumpet will signal the conclusion of the divine mystery:

"When he shall begin to sound, the mystery of God should be finished" (Revelation 10:7), and His Voice will resonate with great triumph. In this profound moment, those resting in the dust will hear the proclamation of the Archangel, who announces:

"You should give rewards to Your servants, the prophets, and to the saints, and those who fear Your Name, both small and great." (Revelation 11:18)

This divine announcement marks the culmination of God's Plan and the ultimate fulfillment of His promises. As *"the Earth casts out the dead"* who were in the depths of Sheol, the faithful, who have long awaited this moment, will awaken to sing praises and stand in awe of Yahweh's magnificent works. It is a day of reward, where justice is served, and the righteous are honored.

The triumphant sound of the Trumpet ushers in the end of suffering and the beginning of a new era of eternal joy for those who have remained true to Jesus unto death. They emerge from their graves, winning the ultimate victory over death and evil.

For those who had endured until the end, standing up for Jesus, He returns to bestow His reward upon them. One of His promises kept:

"To him that overcomes, I will give to eat from the Tree of Life, which is in the midst of the Paradise of God." (Revelation 2:7)

The Tree of Life, initially lost, is restored to bring life and healing to the nations. This is the Paradise where Jesus meets the thief, as they embrace for the first time in fulfillment of the

Savior's promise. The significance of this promise is profound. The Tree of Life, once out of reach due to humanity's fall, is now restored in the renewal of God's creation.

Those who have stood firm in their faith through trials and persecution are rewarded with eternal life and healing from this Divine tree. The privilege of eating from the Tree of Life in a new, immortal body, with no possibility of dying again, and communing with God face-to-face ushers in joy unspeakable and full of glory.

The culmination of God's Redemptive Plan is now realized, where the faithful are not only forgiven but also honored and restored to a place of eternal peace and ecstatic happiness, with another promise now fulfilled:

"You will rejoice in your inheritance. And so, you will inherit a double portion in your land, and everlasting joy will be yours." (Isaiah 61:7)

Picture a joy that will never go away. More importantly, death no longer has dominion over the saints:

"To him that overcomes, I will give the Crown of Life," and "shall not be hurt by the Second Death." (Revelation 2:10-11)

The victory of steadfast faithfulness and the ultimate rewards for unwavering devotion are recognized. The righteous avoided the *"Second Death"* and received a *"Crown of Life,"* a divine affirmation of their consecration and sacrifices. This crown is not merely a symbol but a tribute to their endurance and victory over the Devil's devices, contemplating a profound promise of everlasting life and direct Honor from Yeshua's Hand.

The courageous believers who sacrificed their lives bearing witness to their Savior will enter a world no longer influenced by evil; these valiant souls have conquered the evil one, not by their strength but:

"They overcame him by the Blood of the Lamb and by the word of their testimony, and they did not love their lives to the death." (Revelation 12:11)

The victorious faithful will rise to receive rewards beyond their wildest dreams. Jesus brings the reward with Him to each person according to their actions. The realization of living forever is a reward that surpasses all human understanding.

All of God's Promises are now manifested one after another:

"To him who overcomes I will grant to sit with Me on My Throne, as I also overcame and sat down with My Father on His Throne." (Revelation 3:21)

"To him who overcomes," those who were warriors in their faith, Jesus grants the incredible honor of sitting with Him on His Throne. Imagine the saints honored to share thrones with Jesus—a privilege reserved exclusively for the Overcomers!

All the agony and suffering endured for their faithfulness are elevated to a position that even the unfallen world could not obtain. Imagine this if you can. What a profound recognition and an eternal honor bestowed upon those who had remained faithful to God throughout their journey.

Such a privilege is about victory and, more importantly, an intimate union with Yeshua—sitting on the Throne and sharing in His Authority, Glory, and Triumph. It's an eternal testament to remind believers that their perseverance is recognized and rewarded at the highest level. This promise of co-reigning with Yeshua reflects the depth of His Love and the magnitude of the honor He showers on those who overcome life's trials and remain loyal to Him; what an awe-inspiring destiny awaits those who remain faithful to the end!

Many of those sing a new song that no one knew except those who endured the *"time of trouble such as never was."* A special place is reserved for them, a distinguished group who have emerged from the *"great tribulation" (Revelation 7:14).* These individuals have made their robes white by washing them in the Blood of the Lamb. The revelator unveils their extraordinary reward:

"Therefore, they are before the Throne of God and serve Him day and night in His Temple. And He who sits on the Throne will dwell among them. They shall neither hunger anymore nor thirst anymore; the sun shall not strike them, nor any heat; for the Lamb who is in the midst of the Throne will shepherd them and lead them to living fountains of waters. And God will wipe away every tear from their eyes." (Revelation 7:15-17)

This unique group, honored with the privilege of life without end, comprises those who have triumphed through unparalleled trials and tribulations. Their experiences set them apart and mark them as overcomers, awarding them a place of closeness to God.

The scene depicted here is one of profound comfort and eternal peace. It foretells the transformation from earthly suffering to heavenly bliss. The Lamb, who once sacrificed Himself for humanity, now Shepherds these souls, ensuring they experience no more hunger, thirst, or suffering.

God's wiping away every tear embodies an end to all sorrows and suffering. Life's pains and troubles will, one day, be remembered no more. Imagine Yahweh's Hand wiping away the tears resulting from our grief and tragedies.

One day, those confined to wheelchairs and walkers will *"jump and leap for joy,"* with bodies transformed to immortality! As they jump, leap, and shout, all memories of tragedy and trial will fade away. As it is written:

"Then the lame will leap like a deer, and the mute tongue will shout for joy. For waters will gush forth in the wilderness, and streams in the desert." (Isaiah 35:6)

Imagine the sheer joy and freedom these individuals will experience as they live without physical limitations. Their rejoicing will be so profound that the sorrows and sighs of the past will fade into distant memories. No longer will they journey through the desert wilderness in thirst. This transformation is beautifully captured in the promise:

"And the ransomed of the LORD shall return, and come to Zion with songs and everlasting joy upon their heads: they shall obtain joy and gladness, and sorrow and sighing shall flee away." (Isaiah 35:10)

Suffering and pain will be replaced by a joy we cannot escape. The anticipation of such an incredible transformation provides a powerful reminder of hope and promise that every limitation and sorrow will be wiped away. No more electric bills, car payments, or credit card debt! The sighing every month will give way to laughter and joy. One day, stress will go away.

The Prophet Isaiah presents a stunning portrayal of a world transformed by divine peace and knowledge:

"The wolf shall dwell with the lamb; the leopard shall lie down with the young goat; the calf and the young lion and the fatling together; and a little child shall lead them. The cow and the bear shall graze; their young ones lie together, and the lion shall eat straw like an ox. The nursing child shall play by the cobra's hole,

and the weaned child shall put his hand in the viper's den. They shall not hurt or destroy in all My Holy Mountain; for the Earth shall be full of the knowledge of Yahweh." (Isaiah 11:6-9)

This picture is nothing short of breathtaking. Imagine the natural predators of the animal world coexisting peacefully. Predators and prey, historically at odds, co-exist in perfect harmony. Imagine a child leading and playing among the once untamed animals in a world where fear and danger are no longer present. A place where even the most vulnerable are safe and can play with what were once dangerous creatures. Wow – a child playing around with a Cobra?

This prophecy paints a picture of hope, where chaos and conflict give way to serenity and mutual respect. That is such good news to hope for in such a troubled world: no more school shootings, suicides, homicides, wars, famines, or fears of what the next day will bring.

There will be a world of complete restoration, a future where knowledge and understanding of God saturate every corner of existence, ushering in a serene and harmonious existence for all creation. Can we imagine having the security and confidence to leave our homes without fear of being mugged?

"Behold, I will make all things new." (Revelation 21:5). The old will be replaced with the new. It presents an exhilarating vision where all that has been broken or marred by sin and suffering is fully restored. This new creation transcends a mere return to an Edenic state; it advances us to a realm where God's Presence is fully realized, and His People experience new horizons, new heights, and even a new name:

HELL'S PROPHECY

"The nations shall see Your Righteousness, and all the Kings Your Glory, and you shall be called by a new name that the Mouth of Yahweh will give." (Isaiah 62:2)

This vision of renewal encourages us to look beyond our present trials and hold onto the hope of a future where every aspect of Creation is renewed and reconciled. It invites us to envision a world where Yahweh's Perfect Plan is fulfilled. One day, I hope that I will reunite with my two sons, who passed from this life way too early.

No matter how dire our current circumstances may seem, there is a promised time for renewal and restoration. This transformation is a Divine Guarantee that every wrong will be made right and every sorrow will turn into joy. Holding onto these promises will help us navigate the challenges of today with faith and anticipation for the unimaginable, glorious future that awaits us. It is written:

"In that day, the deaf will hear the words of the book, and the eyes of the blind will see out of obscurity and darkness. The humble will also increase their joy in Yahweh, and the poor among men will rejoice in the Holy One of Israel. The ruthless will come to nothing, the scornful will be consumed, and all who watch for iniquity will be cut off." (Isaiah 29:18-20)

What a happy day when the heartless, merciless, and cruel disappear; the scornful mockers and scoffers will be consumed by fire. All those who hope for the worst in everything, the pessimists and joy-suckers, will be cut off from the Kingdom of Bliss. Why? Because they would not be happy in a place where everyone is ecstatic.

On the other hand, those who are hard of hearing will discard their hearing aids; people experiencing poverty will be joyous because money will no longer be necessary. They will rejoice in the Great Almighty, who will provide for all their needs. The School of the Blind will close its doors. They will then understand as it is written:

"Eye has not seen, nor ear heard, neither has entered into the heart of man, the things which God has prepared for them that love Him." (1 Corinthians 2:9)

Can we truly comprehend what lies ahead? Not fully. We can only glimpse a fraction with our limited vision. But in the New Earth, we will be in awe of the beauty and surprises that await those who believe in Yeshua. We are told that, right now, we see through a dark glass, but one day, we can be assured of many impressive, eye-opening wonders in the days that await us:

"Behold a King shall reign in Righteousness, and princes in Judgment. And man shall be as a hiding place from the wind and a covert from the tempest; as rivers of water in a dry place, as the shadow of a great rock in a weary land. And the eyes of them that see shall not be dim, and the ears of them that hear shall be attentive. The heart also of the rash shall understand knowledge, and the tongue of the stammerers shall be ready to speak plainly." (Isaiah 32:1-4)

One day, we will finally follow a Righteous King of Integrity whom we can trust. His Name is Yeshua, and His Name will be above every name. We will follow His Way, His Truth, and His Life. People will no longer be spiritually or morally blind but will have clarity and discernment. Wisdom will replace impulsiveness, and those who struggle to communicate will express themselves clearly and confidently. Under His Righteous Rule, individuals will find safety, comfort, and their needs met.

Jerusalem, long a place of conflict and conquest by its surrounding enemies, will finally be transformed into its original design as *"The City of Peace."* Isaiah vividly paints this transformation, saying:

"Behold, I create new Heavens and a new Earth, and the former shall not be remembered or come to mind. But be glad and rejoice forever in what I Create... joy in My people, the voice of weeping will no longer be heard" (Isaiah 65:17-19).

The old war-torn Jerusalem will be transformed anew:

"Now I saw a new Heaven and a new Earth, for the first heaven and the first earth had passed away. Also, there was no more sea. I saw the Holy City, New Jerusalem, coming down from heaven from God, prepared as a bride adorned for her husband.

And I heard a Great Voice out of Heaven saying, Behold, the Tabernacle of God is with men, and He will Dwell with them, and they shall be His People, and God Himself shall be with them, and be their God. (Revelation 21:1-3)

Jerusalem will become a symbol of peace where the Father and Son reside. The New Jerusalem is portrayed as a Great City made of the most precious stones and streets of transparent gold. The Father and Son rule together and dwell with us without obstruction.

"The work of righteousness will be peace, and the effect of righteousness, quietness, and assurance forever. My People will dwell in peaceful habitation, secure dwellings, and quiet resting places" (Isaiah 32:17-18).

Imagine a land without a homicide detective, where one can feel secure in leaving all their belongings out in the open, with no sirens blaring in their ears. No more caskets, graveyards, or funeral homes. Emergency rooms, Hospitals, and high-priced health care have vanished. Consider this: Peace in a peaceful palace!

Violence shall no longer be heard in your land, nor shall there be wasting or destruction within your borders. But you shall call your walls 'Salvation' and your gates' Praise.' The sun shall no longer be your light by day, nor the brightness moon withdraw itself, for Yahweh will be your Everlasting Light, and the days of your mourning shall be ended. Also, your people shall all be righteous.

They shall inherit the land forever. The Branch of My Planting, the Work of My Hands, that I may be Glorified. Your sun shall no longer go down, a little one shall become a thousand, and a small one will be a strong nation. I, Yahweh, will hasten it in its time." (Isaiah 60:18-22)

"They shall build houses and inhabit them. They shall plant vineyards and eat their fruit. They shall not build, and another inhabit. They shall not plant and another eat. For as the days of a tree, so shall be the days of My People.

My Elect shall long enjoy the work of their hands. They shall not labor in vain, nor bring forth children for trouble; they will be the descendants of the Blessed of Yahweh, and their children with them." (Isaiah 65:23)

Yahweh will return humanity to the Garden, a place of enjoyment for our work and raising children back to His Original Design and Purpose. According to His Promise, the ones that looked for *"new Heavens and a new Earth"* experience the unspeakable joy, *"where righteousness dwells."* (2 Peter 3:13)

Just think, all the troublemakers are gone, no more obnoxious drunkards to shout obscenities, no drug dealers, no more gangs, no more bullies, no more sex traffickers. On that Day, the righteous are vindicated:

"Behold all those who were incensed against you shall be ashamed and disgraced, they shall be as nothing, and those who strive with you shall perish. You shall seek them and not find them. Those who contend with you, those who war against you, shall be as nothing, as a nonexistent thing." (Isaiah 41: 11-12)

According to this Scripture, we will one day look for these evildoers, and they will *be as nothing*. They will *perish* and *no longer exist* — goodbye and good riddance.

How the Hell?

The Day of Judgment will bring every offender face to face with the Righteous Judge. As Revelation states:
"I saw a Great White Throne, and Him who sat upon it, from whose face the Earth and the heaven away. There was found no place for them. And I saw the dead, both small and great, stand before God." (Revelation 20:11-12)

On that day, equality and justice will be administered by the One who Judges *"with righteousness and decides with equity" (Isaiah 11:4).* Those who died without hope will be raised in the final Resurrection to stand before the Great Almighty. The power of choice is now fully realized. They all stand in line – *"the number of them is as the sand of the sea."*

Buddhists face the reality that their chants and reverence for Buddha cannot shield them from the sight of the Holy God. As they gaze upon Him in His proper form, they will recognize that bowing down to a false image could not save them. Now, it is too late to acknowledge and confess faith in the One who shed His Blood to redeem them from their godless practices and religion.

Muslims who denied the Crucifixion and Resurrection of Yeshua will be in shock when they see the *"King of Kings and the Lord of Lords"* face to Face. Those who expected to be in the presence of 72 virgins after fighting the infidels will realize that their religious pursuit was misguided. They will now behold the Face of Him from whom *"the Heavens and the Earth fled away."* The jihadists and their Prophet will bow to Him, whom they denied as their Lord and Savior. They will find out too late that

Yeshua was God's Son. The bowing of the knee and confessing is too late for them.

With religious pretension stripped away, the hypocrites rise to the wrong Resurrection. No longer can the corrupt priest hide behind the pulpit while committing vile acts. Those who amassed fortunes from the generosity of their congregations to buy airplanes and build empires now stand before God to give an account of their stewardship. One of the haunting questions they will have to ask themselves:

"Lord, when did we see you hungry, or thirsty, or a stranger, or naked, or sick, or in prison, and did not minister to You?" (Matthew 25:44)

All those religious individuals who claimed to be doctrinally correct are now judged not by what they knew to be accurate but by how they met the needs of the less fortunate. Those who divided the churches over theological differences, engaged in argumentative Bible studies, and took pride in their doctrinal distinctives will gnash their teeth in fear before His Righteous Judgment.

Church leaders who mislead their assemblies to believe that God and salvation can only be found in their church will discover that Yahweh is more significant than a building. Denominationalism will vanish in the Sight of the Almighty's Divine Justice. It will become shockingly clear that many other denominational leaders who taught a false gospel are in the same place: the Second Resurrection. Oh, what a tooth-grinding day that will be.

False teachers who secretly infiltrated churches will face stricter condemnation for leading others away from obedience to Yahweh's Holy Law. His Ten Commandments, kept in His

How the Hell?

Temple in Heaven, will shine forth from the *"Ark of His Testament" (Revelation 11:19)*. When Judged by the *"Law of Liberty" (James 2:12)*, it becomes clear that what was written in stone had never been inscribed in their hearts.

Many will come on that Day boasting:

"Lord, Lord, have we not prophesied in Your Name, cast out demons in Your Name, and done many wonders in Your Name?" (Matthew 7:22). The pretenders will hear the terrifying words of condemnation, *"Depart from Me, you who practice lawlessness." (Matthew 7:23)*

Those who preached a "no law-all grace" doctrine realize too late that they cannot transform from doers of iniquity to law-abiding citizens of the Kingdom.

One often-ignored Commandment (the 4th) will shine brightly in the Light of His Judgment out of Yahweh's government of Love. The ones entrusted to teach the Word of God who disregarded the Commandment that specifically identifies Him who *"Made the Heavens, the Earth, the Sea, and all that is in them" (Exodus 20:8-11)* will realize too late that the Seventh Day remains etched in stone as a remembrance of His Authority as Creator.

They bow their heads in shame as they discover that no change in the Day or their theological debates can argue against it. The mouths of false teachers will be silenced as the truth regarding His *"Holy Day" (Isaiah 58:13)* is revealed. What man was commanded to remember had been ignored or forgotten.

Those who, in the Name of God, forced people into slavery, killed heretics, and used violence to eliminate unbelievers will finally see God as He truly is. They will recognize that *"God is*

Love," "a Defender of the Poor and Fatherless," and the Righteous Law Giver.

Counting religious beads, reciting repetitive phrases, and bowing to graven images in the Church will all be exposed in the Light of a Holy God. It will be too late to change the misguided belief that Almighty Yahweh was pleased with such religious nonsense.

Ordained homosexual clergy will gnash their teeth in fear before Him who created Adam and Eve, not Adam and Steve. Those churches that voted in these ministers, recognizing their actions as evil, will realize they are complicit:

"Knowing the Righteous Judgment of God, that those who practice such things are worthy of death, not only doing the same but also approving of those who practice them" (Romans 1:32). Homosexual ministers will be cast out, along with the adoration of those who were led by the lie.

The most vile and atrocious figures in history, who led millions to their deaths—Hitler, Stalin, Mao Zedong, Nero, and countless others—wait at the back of the Judgment Line. They watch those multitudes before they are cast into the Lake of Fire. The Almighty has a special reward for the merciless. As much as humanity suffered from their lawless deeds, vengeance now comes in a fury upon those most deserving of death's solution.

God will impart a punishment especially designed for the most sinister. Whatever God decides their punishment should be, the vilest will receive even greater condemnation when He judges them, in whatever way He chooses to implement it.

God is Just: *"It is a righteous thing with God to repay with tribulation those who trouble you"* (2 Thess 1:6). Payback has arrived.

How the Hell?

Atheists will be in shock, their mouths silenced by the most terrifying image of the Invisible God. Seeing God will make them believers, but it is far too late. They could clearly see His *invisible attributes in the things that were made,* but devised flimsy excuses not to acknowledge their Maker.

"They did not glorify Him as God or give thanks. Instead, they became futile in their thoughts, and their foolish hearts were darkened. Professing to be wise, they became fools (Romans 1:20-22).

Because of their foolish philosophies, *"God gave them up to uncleanness, in the lusts of their hearts...who exchanged the truth of God for the lie." (Romans 1:24)*

Imagine the scene: a sudden, overwhelming realization sweeps over them as they stand before the Almighty. They are now so angry that their teeth are gnashing uncontrollably. All their arguments against God and denials crumble in the face of undeniable truth. The stark contrast between their professed wisdom and the reality of their folly becomes painfully clear.

This profound reckoning exposes the depth of their error and the tragic consequences of rejecting the Creator. Their choices hang heavy as they confront the eternal reality they once denied. They have forfeited their everlasting life.

The schoolteachers who taught God's children the lie that our ancestors came from monkeys - will scream in fear as they face the Holy God they denied. As he looks down on their wretched, trembling bodies, they realize the gravity of their error.

Their worship of the creature rather than the Creator brings a clear revelation as they see the wickedness around them. They understand their guilt in teaching evolution and the chaos it has unleashed among the multitudes standing before them.

HELL'S PROPHECY

Those who were condemned had been:

"Filled with all unrighteousness, sexual immorality, wickedness, covetousness, maliciousness, full of envy, murder, strife, deceit, evil-mindedness, whispering, backbiting, hatred of God, violence, pride, boasting, inventing evil things, disobedience to parents, lack of understanding, untrustworthiness, lack of love, unforgiveness, and lack of mercy."

(Romans 1:26-31).

Men committing shameful acts with men are included, as *"all who practice such things are deserving of death."*

Oh, the weeping and wailing that will echo through the heavens as they realize they have been raised in the wrong resurrection alongside those who deserve nothing but death-no more, no less.

The Second Death

"Blessed and holy is the one who has been raised in the First Resurrection, upon which the Second Death has no power."

— *(Revelation 20:6)*

The Bible teaches that there will be two distinct Resurrections. The saved will receive eternal life, while the unsaved will face a *"Second Death."* For the unrighteous, death will be the last answer.

This marks Yahweh's concluding chapter, where all traces of evil will be burned up and eradicated forever. No one who had rebelled against their Creator can now escape the power of the Second Death—only those empowered by Yeshua.

It seems fitting to raise the wicked once more after they die, allowing them to glimpse the eternal bliss they will miss, where *"the wolf and the lamb will feed together"* and where the prisoner of death is set free.

Since the reward for a wicked person is *"the Second Death,"* it only makes sense - they must die, be raised again, and die once more. However, those who overcome and remain faithful to God *"shall not be hurt by the Second Death."* (Revelation 2:11)

Imagine the profound realization of the rebellious who, standing on the cusp of eternity, sees the serene and joyous future that is forever out of reach. The closed door into the promised Paradise haunts them with the ultimate consequence of their choices. They hear the Judge declare, "Guilty as Charged."

The Second Death

The Sentence – *"The Lake of Fire, which is the Second Death."*

Humanity was forewarned of the consequences of not walking with their Creator in obedience to the faith and the offer of Salvation through His Beloved Son Yeshua. Having provided everything necessary for their redemption, they rejected His Offer and went their way. Insulted by their hardened hearts, He allowed their bad choices to determine their eternity.

The Guilty offenders are now listed and hear their sentences:

"But cowards who turn away from Me, and unbelievers, and the corrupt, and murderers, and the sexually immoral, those who practice witchcraft, idol worshippers, and all liars will have their doom in the Lake that burns with fire and sulfur. This is the Second Death." (Revelation 21:8)

Imagine the gravity of this moment: those who have turned away from Yahweh, who have lived in defiance of His Commandments, facing the finality of *the Second Death*. The Fire Lake, burning with unquenchable flames, is the ultimate consequence of their choices.

Understand there is no "second chance," nor does it describe the Lake of Fire as the "second Hell." This is not about another opportunity for redemption; it is the end of the line, where the full weight of Yahweh's Divine Judgment is felt.

Let's break down the list of the unaccepted into Yahweh's Kingdom: No *cowards*, no *unbelievers*, no *corrupt* individuals, no *sexually immoral* people, no *practitioners of witchcraft*, no *idolaters*, no *murderers*, and finally, *no liars* will live on forever. Now is the time to eradicate evil, destroy sin, and vanquish the devil's works.

The *cowards* who spat vicious curses at God when their faith was tested, those who denied Him out of fear of losing their lives, those who lacked the bravery to stand with the millions who shed their blood as faithful witnesses, and those who ran and hid, never to return to the Almighty, now find themselves raised in true terror as they face the Fiery Lake. He died a coward, was raised still a coward, and dies once more as a coward.

In this moment of ultimate reckoning, the reality of their choices is laid bare. The fear that once drove them to abandon their faith becomes frightening beyond shocking as they face the King of Kings to give an account.

The finality of their fate accentuates the gravity of standing firm in one's beliefs, even in the face of fear and adversity. The Almighty had called them to be witnesses. Now, it is past their allotted time to speak except to weep and wail.

The *unbelievers* who laughed at the idea of Yeshua being the Savior of the world, who died scoffing, are raised from the dead, still scoffing. They would not believe in the Son of Yahweh but proclaimed that many paths would lead to God Almighty. Those who rejected Jesus during His Ministry on earth weep and wail when they see that what He said would happen has happened just as He said it would.

Those who did not believe and mocked Yeshua's Offer were gathered from the dead to be burned up in another death, a second one. As they behold the One with whom they denied, it will surely be "Hell" for them. The unbeliever went down to the grave as an unbeliever and rose from the grave, believing - a little too late.

The *corrupt* who defiled themselves for money, who stole millions from the vulnerable and trusting, who died ripping off the multitudes with scams, identity theft, and crooked politics, and all who sold out their integrity to gain wealth by fraud are

The Second Death

raised for their eternal sentencing. Now, their money cannot save them from the snare of the Second Death. Instead of counting their money, they now count their deaths – times two.

In this terrifying moment, the profound reality of their choices becomes undeniable. The wealth they once valued so highly is rendered meaningless in the Face of Yahweh's Free Grace. What folly is material gain at the expense of integrity, which leads to eternal consequences? What had it profited them to gain the whole world and find out they had lost their soul? It was too late to discover that the worship of money was the root of all evil.

The *murderers* who took the lives of the innocent and bystanders, those who killed the unborn, those who executed hundreds of thousands without cause in the wars, the serial killers, and those responsible for the genocide of millions will rise from the ground to face the most agonizing death.

There is no eternal life for the murderer—just a death twice over in a fire that consumes everything to nothing. Those who killed the bodies of men are now killed by the One who destroys both body and soul, delivered as promised: a terrible death two times.

Nowhere in all of Scripture can one find a verse supporting the idea that a deathless, miserable, evil soul is granted immortality. A diligent Bible student will not find a single verse declaring that a murderer possesses an immortal soul. On the contrary, the disciple John states,

"No murderer has eternal life abiding in him" (1 John 3:15). Life in eternity is not possible for the soul of a serial killer, child killer, or cold-blooded murderer. There is no eternal torment here, sorry, little devil.

HELL'S PROPHECY

In this moment of Divine Calculation, the weight of their evil deeds becomes undeniable. Their heinous deeds are met with the most severe consequences. Those who had no regard for life, those who had shed innocent blood, now stand before the One who shed His Blood in innocence to redeem them from their sin and Judgment. Rejected - they also become rejected.

Imagine the scene: the sky darkens, and a profound silence falls over the multitudes. The ground trembles as the Righteous Judge speaks, echoing through the Heavens and the Earth. The cursed, with faces twisted in fear and regret, are cast into the Lake of Fire, where the flames of Divine Justice burn them up.

The air is thick with the weight of finality as the reality of their fate sinks in. The unquenchable and all-consuming fire testifies to the ultimate consequence of rebellion against the Almighty. This is when Divine Order is fully realized, and the eternal separation from Yahweh is sealed.

The *sexually immoral*, the perverts, the gays, transgender people, swingers, those who participated in making pornography, the enslaved millions addicted to its alluring bondage, the rapist, and all fornicators wake up to the sight of a Pure Holy God.

The God of Justice brings down the Judgment, the fire of eternal death. They died a pervert, raised a pervert, destroyed in another death - no more pervert. As God cast the pleasure seekers into the fire, He *takes no pleasure in the death of the wicked.*

The witches, those practicing white magic and black magic, tarot card readers, mediums, fortunetellers, palm readers, new age channelers, astrologers, Satan worshippers, ghost chasers, spell casters, voodoo practitioners, and all others who trusted in

The Second Death

esoteric rituals will find that their "reincarnation" was a Resurrection—the second one. They will not deliver themselves from the power of the flame. There will be no escaping the Second Death for them.

The reality of their choices becomes undeniable. The esoteric practices they once relied on are powerless against the Righteous Judgment they now face. The finality of the Second Death reinforces the seriousness of their actions and the futility of seeking power outside of God's Truth. This profound moment serves as a sober reminder of the importance of aligning one's life with Divine principles and rejecting the allurement of Satan's devices embodied in false spiritual pursuits.

The *idolaters,* those who spent their whole lives worshipping things, will find themselves raised in a Resurrection to see God as He truly is. The bowing down to the images of Buddha, Mary, the mother of Jesus, venerated saints, Krishna, the Holy Cows, statues of the Greek gods, Sun worshippers, and all who likened God to anything made - will now bow down to the invisible God made visible. As He casts them into the Fiery Lake, they face another death. Do the math: one plus one equals two. That is how many times the Bible declares that the idolater will die.

Oh, one more on the list—*the liar.* The ones who misled multitudes to believe lies, who twisted the truth, stretched it just a little; those who taught half-truths, three-quarter truths, fifteen-sixteenths truths; the false teachers of evolution, those teaching false doctrines leading many away from the faith of God; those who made lying a habit, and those who in the name of righteousness lied while doing wrong - now recognize what Satan's said: *"You will not surely die,"* as a colossal lie.

HELL'S PROPHECY

These deceptive actions are fully exposed at this instant of Divine Calculation. The fire of Yahweh's Judgment consumes the lies they once propagated, leaving no more room for deceit. The finality of the Second Death is a powerful reminder of the importance of truth and integrity. Those who twisted the truth and misled others will face the eternal consequences of their actions.

On that Day, the most terrifying words will happen:

"Depart from me; you cursed into the everlasting fire prepared for the devil and his angels."

It has been decreed that the Devil and his loyal angelic followers will experience the Fire of Yahweh. *"These will go away into everlasting punishment"* (Matthew 25:46), not everlasting *punishing*. Whatever the punishment, it will last forever and ever.

So, what exactly is the Second Death? In this passage, it is described a little differently:

"These are the hidden reefs, feasting together with you fearlessly in your love feasts; shepherding themselves; clouds without water, being carried about by winds; autumnal trees without fruit, twice having died, having been uprooted." (Jude 1:6)

Have you ever heard of the phrase *"Twice having died"*?

For most etymologists and mathematicians, this would be an obvious calculation. When the Book of Revelation speaks of the *"Second Death"* four times, it should be noted as a matter of extreme importance and significance. Each time the Prophet mentions the phrase, it alludes to a final event. Having been thrown into the Lake of Fire, the unrighteous experience a Second Death.

The Second Death

It is only those who believe that death is not death who can produce the *"living dead"* in the Hell scenario. Let us not read something in the text that is not there. As you have discovered, the support for eternal conscious torment is a big stretch from the actual truth.

Hell No More

"For the wicked will be destroyed...in a little while, the wicked will disappear; though you look for them, they will be gone... But the wicked shall perish... into smoke, they will vanish away."

(Psalm 37:10, 20)

Israel's King received insight from God concerning the fate of the wicked. The language used in these passages—*destroyed, perished, vanished away*—indicates that the wicked will be *no more*. Evil will come to an end. Although the wicked may seem to prosper for a time, their end is inevitable. The vision of the wicked vanishing like smoke signifies wickedness's complete and utter end. King David continues:

"I have seen the wicked in great power... yet he passed away, and behold—he is no more. Indeed, I sought him, but he could not be found... " The transgressors shall be destroyed together; the future of the wicked shall be cut off" (Psalm 37:36, 38).

If there is no future for evil to remain, evil people will not squirm throughout eternity. Do we have to wonder what *"destroyed"* means in this revelation? Again, looking up the meaning in a dictionary would be beneficial.

"For the transgressors shall be destroyed together, the future of the wicked will be cut off ...When the wicked are cut off, you shall see it." (Psalm 37:28, 34)

According to this verse, the wicked will not live eternally; their future will ultimately end. When a head is *"cut off"* from a body, there is no more life. There is no future in eternity for anything cut off from its life source. For the cut-off, there will be no future - period. Those who turn away from righteousness will face an irrevocable end. The wicked will not persist forever; their time is finite, and their end is inevitable.

"You cast them down to destruction; how they are brought to desolation as in a moment." (Psalm 73:17)

Carefully examining this passage helps us understand that bringing the wicked to desolation does not take an eternity. Desolation will occur in "just *a moment.*" Destruction and desolation will be the lot of those cast down. "*Desolate*" is defined as *vacant, uninhabited, and unoccupied*. Is Hell really as full as some say it is?

"God shall likewise destroy you forever. He shall take you away, and pluck you up out of your dwelling place, and uproot you from the land of the living." (Psalm 52:5)

Have you ever seen anything "*plucked up*" from the ground live very long? Most gardeners would agree that life ends when something is uprooted. How can anyone ignore the sentencing of the harmful plants: "*destroyed foreve*r?" Some call it '*eternal destruction.*' It sure seems odd to think of eternal torture as a reality when examining these clear-cut passages.

The analogy to gardening makes it clear that those who are cut off from the source of life have no chance of survival or a future. This is a powerful reminder of the consequences of turning away from righteousness and the importance of being connected to the source of life. Yeshua is the Vine.

"When the wicked spring as the grass, and when all the workers of iniquity do flourish, it is that they will be destroyed forever..." Surely, your enemies shall perish." (Psalm 92:7,9)

Again, just what does the phrase *"destroyed forever"* mean? How about the word *"perish?"* Join the phrase *"everlasting destruction"* with these words. What do you produce? It will be the effects of destruction that will last forever. Has anyone ever looked up the word *perish*? Outer darkness takes on a whole new meaning.

As one searches through the Word of God, it becomes apparent that wickedness does have an end in mind. Consider this passage from another Bible prophet:

"The destruction of transgressors and sinners shall be together, and those who forsake Yahweh will be consumed...So, the Light of Israel will be for a fire... It will burn and devour... both body and soul." (Isaiah 1:28; 10:17-18)

This Prophet very clearly articulated that "*both body and soul*" together will be burned and devoured. There is no hint whatsoever of an eternal Hell where the wicked will be able to fornicate forever. The destruction that *devours* provides the concluding answer to evil. The prophet's words mandate that wickedness will face destruction without lingering forever in an eternal fire hole.

This same Prophet foretold a time when even the coals of fire would turn cold! He declares:

"Let now the astrologers, the stargazers, and the monthly prognosticators stand up and save you. Behold, they shall be as stubble; the fire shall burn them. They shall not deliver themselves from the power of the flame. There shall not be a warm coal or a fire to sit before." (Isaiah 47:13-14)

After the fire burns the wicked to stubble, it goes out—and there will not be one warm coal left to sit in front of! This passage reveals the ultimate futility of relying on false sources of salvation. Once seeking guidance and protection, astrologers, stargazers, and prognosticators cannot save themselves from the consuming fire. The imagery of the fire burning to stubble and then going out contradicts the eternal conscious torment.

"Lift up your eyes to the heavens and look on the Earth beneath. For the heavens will vanish away like smoke, the Earth will grow old like a garment, and those who dwell in it will die in like manner." (Isaiah 51:6)

Underneath the heavens, Earth dwellers will die and disappear as the sky vanishes—there will be no roasting and toasting forever here. The heavens vanishing like smoke and the Earth growing old like a garment signify the eventual dissolution of the physical world. Similarly, those who dwell on Earth face the same fate: death and disappearance.

Another witness of the Old Testament used vivid imagery, likening the evildoer's fate to:

"A morning mist, early dew that passes away, chaff, and like smoke from a chimney." (Hosea 13:3)

There does not seem to be a hint of fire engulfing the "living dead" unbeliever. On the contrary, all the metaphors, *mists, dew, and chaff* are elements that eventually vanish *into smoke*. Again and again, the Scriptures are in complete harmony regarding the end of evil.

"The wicked shall be turned into Hell (Sheol), and all the nations that forget God... Upon the wicked, He will rain coals; fire and brimstone, and a burning wind shall be the portion of their cup." (Psalm 9:17; 11:6)

This passage paints a terrifying picture: fire and brimstone falling from the sky, raining down on the wicked. No umbrella, no earthly protection will withstand God's fiery judgment. When this Judgment comes, the evil will wish they were underground.

We have a precedent for this "fire rain" in the destruction of Sodom and Gomorrah. Before the return of Yeshua, He likens the end to those days:

"It was the same in the days of Lot. People were eating and drinking, buying and selling, planting and building. But the day Lot left Sodom, fire and sulfur rained down from Heaven and destroyed them all. It will be like this on the day the Son of Man is revealed." (Luke 17:28-30)

In those days, the cities were plagued by acts of same-gender attraction, sexual deviation, and fornication, which brought about Divine Judgment. Today, similar sins are widespread. We must warn them that such sins will bring judgment despite our reluctance to offend others. Just as Sodom was destroyed, so will our world if it continues down this path. The Bible tells us:

*"In like manner, Sodom and Gomorrah and the cities around them, who indulged in sexual immorality and pursued strange flesh, are on display as an example of those who sustain the punishment of **eternal fire**." (Jude 1:7)*

Understanding what *"eternal fire"* means in this context is crucial. Sodom and Gomorrah suffered the vengeance of eternal fire, but this does not mean the fire still burns today. Both cities were turned *into ashes*, serving as an example to the ungodly:

"And turning the cities of Sodom and Gomorrah into ashes, condemned them to destruction, making them an example to those who afterward would live ungodly." (2 Peter 2:6)

Archaeological discoveries of brimstone and ash in the Dead Sea area continue to provide evidence of their destruction. Eternal fire and everlasting fire have the same meaning. If

Sodom and Gomorrah burned up and turned to ashes, the results of the fire were eternal (everlasting).

Everlasting Fire burns up anything in its path, and its effects are irreversible. The above passage exemplifies what will happen to those who live ungodly afterward. They will be turned to ashes, and their fate will be eternal destruction. Like Sodom and Gomorrah, they, too, will suffer the consequences of eternal fire.

The Rich Man and Lazarus

"There was a rich man clothed in purple and fine linen and feasted sumptuously every day. At his gate was a beggar named Lazarus, covered with sores and longing to eat what fell from the rich man's table. Even the dogs came and licked his sores."

"The time came when the beggar died, and the angels carried him to Abraham's side. The rich man also died and was buried. In Hades, where he was in torment, he saw Abraham far away, with Lazarus by his side. So, he called, 'Father Abraham, have pity on me and send Lazarus to dip the tip of his finger in water and cool my tongue because I am in agony in this fire."

But Abraham replied, 'Son, remember that in your lifetime you received your good things, while Lazarus received bad things, but now he is comforted here, and you are in agony. And besides all this, a great chasm has been set in place between us and you so that those who want to go from here to you cannot, nor can anyone, cross over from there to us.

He answered, 'Then I beg you, Father, send Lazarus to my family, for I have five brothers. Let him warn them so they will not come to this place of torment." Abraham replied, "They have Moses and the Prophets; let them listen to them."

"No, Father Abraham," he said, "but if someone from the dead goes to them, they will repent."

"He said to him, 'If they do not listen to Moses and the Prophets, they will not be convinced even if someone rises from the dead." (Luke 16:19 - 31)

This parable has been one of the most misinterpreted stories in the entire Bible. Those who teach about "Hell" regard this parable as a *literal story*. Proponents of Hell use this parable to support their presuppositions about an underworld of eternal torment revolving around the story of a rich man and a man named Lazarus.

In fact, without this story, their entire concept of an underworld of eternal torment would collapse under the weight of other evidence in Scripture about the wicked perishing. I intend to disprove that this parable proves any such thing as eternal conscious Hell.

A parable is a narrative that conveys a moral or spiritual lesson through an illustrative story. These narratives apply everyday events or scenarios to reveal profound truths and ethical teachings. Jesus artfully employed parables in His teachings, transforming complex spiritual ideas into relatable and understandable lessons for His listeners. These parables stimulate deep thought and self-reflection, guiding individuals toward a richer understanding of moral and spiritual principles.

A series of parables offers profound insights into the attitudes held by the religious leaders of Yeshua's time, particularly within the context of the rich man and Lazarus parable.

These parables often began with phrases like "*A certain man...*" *(Luke 15:11),* "*There was a certain rich man...*" *(Luke 16:1), and "There was a certain rich man..." (Luke 16:19).* Each of these parables highlighted the selfish mindsets of the Jewish religious leaders, revealing hard truths about the Kingdom of God and those who would partake in it.

The Rich Man and Lazarus

In one parable, a *"certain rich man"* hoarded his wealth, only to die and leave everything behind *(Luke 12:16-21)*. The moral of this story is clear: the temporary nature of earthly riches causes selfishness and leads to the inevitable consequence of eternal loss.

Often, the Jews were represented allegorically as *rich* men characterized by their selfishness and lack of compassion. These Parables frequently portrayed a stark contrast between outward religiosity and inner moral failings. These stories emphasized the importance of living a life aligned with God's Purpose and Will, vividly illustrating the consequences of failing to do so.

Yeshua's direct teachings often confronted the listeners with uncomfortable truths about their behavior and beliefs. This method was intended to provoke reflection and change.

For those who believe the parable of the rich man and Lazarus is a *literal story*, consider the following points that challenge this interpretation.

Here are some thought-provoking questions that highlight why this parable might not teach the existence of *Heaven* and *Hell* at death.

Does the Scripture teach that because a man is rich, clothed well, and prosperous, it insinuates that all of them are doomed to the torture chamber? Abraham was rich, yet he wound up in a place of comfort. This story must not be interpreted literally.

Otherwise, those with much money are doomed to eternal thirst. If all the rich are fated to torture throughout eternity, then it would be well for those preachers living above the poverty line to go and give away their offerings and become like Lazarus.

Must a person be poor to attain an eternal inheritance? If that were the case, everyone with wealth would need to turn their riches into rags, and all would have to become beggars. Is it necessary for someone to be sick with sores, ignored, and hungry to enter "Abraham's Bosom?" Obviously not.

Do the saved have to be poor and covered in sores to be in the company of all who are saved? Are all those who are rich sinners? Does a poor person automatically reach sainthood? Maybe then all who are Christians should become beggars, starve, and lie around waiting for a place in Abraham's Bosom.

When the righteous die, do they go straight to Abraham's Bosom? Outside of this story, can it be found where angels carry the dead away at death to Abraham? Scripture clearly shows that messengers or angels do not carry those who die to their reward at death. Instead of going to Abraham, the destiny at death is clear:

"You return unto the ground; for out of it were you taken: for dust you are, and unto dust shall you return." (Gen. 3:17-19)

"All go unto one place; all are of the dust, and all return to dust again." (Ecclesiastes 3:18-21)

"Then the dust will return to the earth as it was, and the Spirit will return to God who gave it." (Ecclesiastes 12:7)

"Remember I pray you that as clay you did make me, and unto dust, you will cause me to return." (Job 10:9)

"You cause man to return unto dust..." (Psa. 90:3)

"You take away their breath; they die and return to their dust." (Psa. 104:29)

If this parable is meant to be taken *literally*, then it suggests the redeemed can speak from Heaven to those in Hell and observe torture chambers full of wealthy men. Picture the poor gathered in Abraham's Bosom while the rich man, desperate for relief, begs Lazarus for a drop of water to soothe his tongue. This depiction implies that the body never burns up in God's Consuming Fire.

According to this eye-opening passage:

"The wicked shall perish, and the enemies of Yahweh shall be as the fat of lambs: they shall consume; into smoke shall they consume away." (Psalm 37:20)

The rich man "*died and was buried.*" If the rich man were to die in the fire, he would not be able to speak. Have you ever seen anything put in a fire that did not burn up? The fire would consume the eyes, tongue, and speaking ability. It is the body that is put into the flames for destruction. Remember, Jesus said that *"both body and soul"* will be *destroyed* in Gehenna (Hell). *(Matthew 10:28)*

If the parable is a literal story, could those in Abraham's Bosom touch the tongue of the tormented with a drop of water? What good would a single drop of water do for those suffering in the Lake of Fire? Even if water could be transported to the place of torment, how much relief could a finger dip provide? Moreover, Jesus, not Father Abraham, offers the Living Water that quenches eternal thirst.

If someone in "Hell" (Hades) prays upward, does Father Abraham provide intercession between the lost and the found? What benefit would the rich man gain from appealing to Father Abraham anyway? A dead man cannot mediate for anyone. If mediation were possible, wouldn't Yeshua be the one to reason with and make a bargain? After all:

"There is one God and one Mediator between God and men, the Man Christ Jesus." (1 Timothy 2:5)

HELL'S PROPHECY

Will the eternally redeemed, where *"there will be no more death, nor sorrow, nor crying, neither shall there be any more pain, for the former things have passed away" (Revelation 21:1,4)*, be able to witness others being tortured in the New Heaven and New Earth? God will wipe away all tears from their eyes, never to return. If they were to see others being tormented, would it not bring agony, terror, and tears once more?

This story cannot be taken literally because most proponents of Hell believe that the disembodied soul is alive. If the soul does not have a body, then taking this parable literally contradicts the belief that the soul has no body. The rich man in the parable has eyes and a tongue, while Jesus warned that the "whole body" would be cast into Gehenna. According to the parable of the rich man and Lazarus, those in "Abraham's Bosom" and "Hades" have bodies.

Many believe that those who died and went to heaven are waiting to receive their bodies at the Resurrection. When the Resurrection occurs, these disembodied souls will receive their new bodies. This parable contradicts that assumption. It poses a problem for those who believe in a literal interpretation, as the rich man had eyes and a mouth and wanted Lazarus to reach down with his finger, indicating bodily form.

If those in "Abraham's Bosom" have bodies at death, and those in Hades also receive bodies immediately, and both go straight to their reward at death, then what would be the purpose of a Judgment or Resurrection? Scripture is clear: death first, then Judgment (Hebrews 9:27). This story has no Judgment or resurrection.

The true meaning lies in the story of the "God Squad," who walked around pretending to be righteous and religious. They tithed and observed all the Holy Days. They spoke the words but did not live by them. Their hearts were far from the Messiah. Jesus came to his own, but his own did not receive him.

The rich man in the story represents the Scribes and Pharisees. They lacked compassion, love, and sympathy for people experiencing poverty. They prided themselves on being descendants of Abraham, claiming him as their father. The religious leaders believed they were righteous because they were of Abraham's bloodline. When Jesus told them they needed to be set free:

"They answered Him, 'We are Abraham's descendants and have never been in bondage to anyone.'"

Jesus replied: *"I know that you are Abraham's descendants, but you seek to kill Me because My word has no place in you. They answered and said to Him, "Abraham is our father." Jesus said to them, "If you were Abraham's children, you would do the works of Abraham."* (John 8:33, 37, 39)

In the parable, the poor man Lazarus wound up being with Abraham, and the rich man, who claimed *"Father Abraham"* as their intercessor, wound up reversing roles:

"Abraham *said, Son, remember that thou in thy lifetime received thy good things, and Lazarus in like manner evil things: but now here he is comforted, and you are in anguish."* (Luke 16:25)

Jesus included the name Lazarus in the story for a specific purpose. After the rich man pleaded with Father Abraham for relief from his torment in the flames of Hades, he then asked Abraham to send Lazarus back to his family. He wanted Lazarus to warn them about the consequences of their selfish behaviors and encourage them to change before they faced the same Judgment. His appeal was:

"Then I beg you, Father," he said, "send Lazarus to my father's house, for I have five brothers. Let him warn them so that they will not also end up in this place of torment." (Luke 16:27-28)

At some point, the rich man realized the need for repentance and the urgency of warning others to avoid the same fate. Oftentimes, the urge to do something right comes way too late.

Abraham replied, *"They have Moses and the Prophets; let them listen to them."* The Pharisees, Scribes, and Sadducees possessed the Oracles of Yahweh. The Torah provided all the instructions they needed to understand their duty to *"Love your neighbor as yourself" (Leviticus 19:18).* If they would not listen to the prophets, neither would they listen to Lazarus.

The rich man was convinced that his brothers would listen:

"'No, Father Abraham,' he said, 'but if someone from the dead goes to them, they will repent.' (Luke 16:30)

Father Abraham replied: 'If they do not listen to Moses and the Prophets, they will not be convinced even if someone rises from the dead." (Luke 16:31) That was the end of the dialogue and parable.

You see, the Pharisees were blind to their spiritual condition. They had this "us four-no more" attitude about their own and ignored everyone else. All through their writings in the Torah, they were to show compassion for the poor in the land. However, they were self-centered and looked at everyone else as "dogs."

In those days, dogs were considered unclean animals. The Pharisees had no regard for the unfortunate. Yeshua used the illustration of a dog to liken Lazarus's despicable condition to the rich man's indifference to his circumstances. They rejected

The Rich Man and Lazarus

Moses and the Prophets. Even the dogs licking the poor man's sores illustrated more kindness to the suffering man than the Pharisee's willful ignorance of his need. The rich man believed Lazarus was in good company with the dogs.

The name Lazarus was included in the parable because Yeshua knew that someone named Lazarus would return from the dead after four days in the grave. When Lazarus came back to life, the religious leaders were not only unconvinced, but his resurrection also prompted them to plot the murder of their Messiah.

When Lazarus was raised from the grave, the religious leaders hardened their hearts even further. They realized they could not refute such an apparent miracle that the Messiah Yeshua had manifested in their sight. This miracle became the turning point for their ultimate rejection of Yeshua. They responded by saying:

"You do not realize that it is better for you that one man dies for the people than that the whole nation perishes... Then, from that day on, they plotted to put Him to death." (John 11:50, 53)

Despite witnessing Lazarus's Resurrection, they were not convinced. They brought Jesus before their leaders and persuaded the authorities to put Him to death. They believed Yeshua needed to die so the nation would not perish. Little did they know Jesus would rise from the grave after His Death. Even then, they still did not believe in Him after the Resurrection.

Can you believe the religious leaders' hard-heartedness and determination to maintain their power despite miraculous evidence? How can someone witness a life returning from the dead without being convinced that the One who performed the miracle was Divine? He proclaimed that He was *the Resurrection and the Life* and proved it by raising Lazarus.

The main idea and obvious lesson are this: the rich man represents those who are spiritually poor regardless of their material superiority and religious standing. On the other hand, Lazarus is likened to those who may be materially poor but are spiritually rich because of their faith and trust in God.

This parable urgently challenges us to reflect on our lives, how we treat others, and what being a servant to Yeshua should look like. The parable teaches us to adhere to Jesus' calling for us to be His Hands, Heart, and Mouthpiece.

Faithful followers of Yeshua will not be indifferent to the cause of the poor like the rich man in this narrative. The parable illuminates the hypocrisy of those who pretend to be righteous - but are full of greed and lack of concern for others. Jesus used this story to caution against the dangers of a life driven by selfishness and void of love for the unfortunate.

The parable teaches moral responsibilities to act with compassion and justice. Neglecting the needs of others has severe consequences and has no place in Yahweh's Kingdom. Until such individuals repent and change their ways, they live in a state of self-torment, separated from the true essence of God's Love and Favor. If you miss the point, you will miss out on eternity.

The impassable gulf between the rich man and Lazarus symbolizes the irreversible separation between the righteous and the wicked after death. What you do here will make a big difference there. The goodness or neglect of the poor and unfortunate will be weighed in Judgment at the end. If we have our focus wrong – now is the time for change. We cannot change after we die. Our destiny is sealed.

Remember, God has appointed a Day when *"He will Judge the world in Righteousness" (Acts 17:31)*. Jesus will return to give His Reward. According to our Savior, Judgment will be based on what we do for the hungry, sick, prisoners, and those in need of clothing. Whatever we do—or fail to do—for them, we have done to Jesus.

After death, one's spiritual state is final, with no possibility of crossing over from the fate of the Second Death to Paradise. We must consider the focus of our hearts as we awaken to one of two resurrections.

The parable urges us to understand our calling deeply. Eternal life in *Hades* is not what happens the minute after death. Both the rich man and Abraham had died. If the *"dead do not know anything,"* there can be no conversations or debates. The rich man will have to stand before the Judge first. That is when he can make His plea – indeed, not to Abraham.

No, the parable of the rich man and Lazarus is not literal. It is an eye-opening lesson about getting on with God's business.

Will there be a fire someday? Will there be torment and agony in realizing that you lived your life selfishly? Will there be regret? Will you gnash your teeth in anger when you recognize that you have forfeited the gift of eternal life? Will you want to make excuses? Will you cry like a baby? Count on it.

It is time to understand the accountability part of this story. There will be a day when we are asked, 'What did you do with what I gave you?'

As Yeshua said, *"Work while it is yet day, for the Night is coming when no man will work." (John 9:4)*

Hell No

"Then a war broke out in heaven: Michael and his angels fought against the dragon, and the dragon and his angels fought back. But the dragon was not strong enough, and no longer was any place found in heaven for him and his angels. And the great dragon was hurled down—that ancient serpent called the devil and Satan, the deceiver of the whole world. He was hurled to the Earth, and his angels with him."

(Revelation 12:7-9)

The time has arrived. The age-old battle between good and evil is nearing its conclusion. Sin and rebellion have reached their limit. For far too long, the devil has held significant authority over this Earth. When Adam, the first man, sinned, Satan was given the title of the deed and ownership of the Earth. Yeshua referred to the devil as the *"Prince of this world."*

Yeshua came down from His Heavenly home to eliminate evil and its author. As the Son of Man looked ahead to His journey to the cross, He declared:

"Now Judgment is upon this world; now the Prince of this world will be cast out." (John 12:31)

For thousands of years, the devil has been granted authority and freedom to establish his domain on Earth, deceiving multitudes of followers for a time and a season. However, according to the revelation, the appointed time of Yahweh's Forbearance has ended. The Cup of His Indignation is full. The final battle begins in the Courtroom of the Almighty, and Satan is no longer allowed access before His Throne.

As the war starts in heaven, the devil and his angels are losers; now, they are thrown out and descend to Earth for a final period. Then a loud voice is heard in heaven, proclaiming:

"Now salvation, strength, the Kingdom of our God, and the Power of His Christ have come, for the accuser of our brethren, who accused them before our God day and night, has been cast down." (Revelation 12:10)

The pronouncement follows this: *"Therefore rejoice, you heavens and you who dwell in them! But woe to the Earth and the sea because the devil has gone down to you! He is filled with fury because he knows that his time is short" (Revelation 12:12).*

For those who dwell in heaven, the call to rejoice is clear. However, *woe* to those on Earth, as they become targets of evil's destructive pursuit. The devil is furious because he knows his time is short. The conflict between Yahweh and Satan is nearing its conclusion.

With no devil present, the final work of Judgment begins in Heaven. The Prophet Daniel reveals this awe-struck scene:

"As I looked, Thrones were set in place, and the Ancient of Days took His Seat. His Clothing was as white as snow; the Hair on His Head was white like wool. His Throne was flaming with fire, and its wheels were all ablaze. A fiery stream issued and came forth from before Him. A thousand thousands ministered to Him; Ten thousand times, ten thousand stood before Him. The Court was seated, and the Books were opened." (Daniel 7:9-10)

"I was watching in the night visions, and behold, One like the Son of Man, Coming with the clouds of heaven! He came to the Ancient of Days, and they brought Him near before Him. Then, to

Him, He was given Dominion and Glory and a Kingdom, and all peoples, nations, and languages should serve Him. His Dominion is an everlasting dominion, which shall not pass away, and His Kingdom shall not be destroyed." (Daniel 7:13-14)

After Satan is expelled from heaven, the Judgment of the righteous begins. *"For it is time for Judgment to begin at the household of God" (1 Peter 4:17).* As the Books are opened, the Son of Man enters the Presence of His Father to Advocate for those He purchased with His blood. The victory is signed, sealed, and delivered as He is granted His Everlasting Dominion, which will never be destroyed. At this moment, Yeshua receives a scroll from the Father's Hand, granting Him the Authority to destroy the devil's works.

A succession of Judgments falls on the Earth to rid it of Satan's hold on humanity. Finally, in Yahweh's very last moments of Judgment, His Angel holding the Seventh Trumpet begins to sound:

"Then the Seventh Angel sounded: And there were loud voices in heaven, saying, "The kingdoms of this world have become the Kingdoms of our Lord and His Christ, and He shall reign forever and ever! The nations were angry, and Your Wrath has come, and the time of the dead, that they should be judged, and that You should reward Your servants, the prophets, and the saints, and those who fear Your name, small and great, and should destroy those who destroy the Earth." (Revelation 11:15,18)

As the Bowls of Yahweh's Wrath are poured out on a maddened Earth led by Satan, the final (Seventh) Bowl of Wrath plummets down, obliterating Satan's dominion and authority over the Earth. The Prophet describes it this way: *"From the sky huge hailstones, each weighing about a hundred pounds, fell on people. And they cursed God on account of the plague of hail because the plague was so terrible" (Revelation 16:21).*

After the Precious Son of God unleashes the Judgments on Satan and his domain, the devil is thrown into a "jailhouse" to await sentencing from the Sovereign Judge. The evil angel who led the world into sin is now held accountable. The Messiah's mission to eradicate sin is nearing completion.

To restore the world to His original intent and design, the ultimate goal is explained*: "He who sins is of the devil, for the devil has sinned from the beginning. For this purpose, the Son of God was, that He might destroy the works of the devil" (1 John 3:8).*

Because Adam was granted free will, he chose to disobey his Maker. As a result, the consequence of sin was death. It is written that Yeshua "suffered *death so that by the grace of God, He might taste death for everyone" (Hebrews 2:9).* He took on the death we deserve to redeem us.

Humanity was lost, and Yeshua took on His mission: *"Inasmuch then as the children have partaken of flesh and blood, He likewise shared in the same, that through death, He might destroy him who had the power of death, that is, the devil" (Hebrews 2:14).* Through the Savior's Death and subsequent Resurrection, He emerged victorious having:

"Disarmed the powers and authorities, He made a public spectacle of them, triumphing over them by the cross." (Colossians 2:15)

When Satan had his followers kill the Savior of the world, he was hoping the battle was over. Death could not hold the Messiah, and the devil knew it. Satan knows the Scriptures as well as anyone. Possibly, he was delusional enough at the time to believe the Son of God would stay in His Grave. After three days, Hades could no longer hold the Savior. Victory in Yeshua, our Savior forever.

Here is a crucial thought: Yeshua left the Glory He shared before the world existed, taking on the form of man, born of a virgin, so that He could die and taste death for lost humanity. His mission was to *destroy* Satan, who brought death into reality, *eliminate* his power over humanity, and *eradicate* the chaos he created.

It is puzzling why many believe that Yahweh would allow Satan to continue his chaos and lordship over evil in a private domain called "Hell" forever. After all, God will not let evil continue eternally. What would be the sense of that? Contrary to popular opinion, according to the Scriptures, Yeshua is going to *eliminate* Satan, destroying both him and his works. We might want to re-examine the word "*destroy.*" Every definition associated with this word conveys finality.

Among the many crimes committed by Satan, the Bible reveals his indictment: *"The devil…He was a murderer from the beginning, refusing to uphold the truth because there is no truth in him. When he lies, he speaks his native language, because he is a liar and the father of lies" (John 8:44).* The arrest warrant is issued, and Satan is locked up:

"Then I saw an Angel coming down from heaven, having the key to the bottomless pit and a great chain in his hand. He laid hold of the dragon, that serpent of old, who is the Devil and Satan, and bound him for a thousand years; and he cast him into the bottomless pit, and shut him up, and set a seal on him so that he should deceive the nations no more till the thousand years were finished. But after these things he must be released for a little while" (Revelation 20:1-3).

The Prophet Isaiah hints at the humbling of the devil in what is described in the pit:

"Hell (Sheol) from beneath is excited about you, to meet you at your coming; It stirs up the dead for you, all the chief ones of the Earth; It has raised from their thrones all the kings of the nations. They all shall speak and say to you: "Have you also become as weak as we? Have you become like us? Your pomp is brought down to Sheol, and the sound of your stringed instruments; The maggot is spread under you, and worms cover you." (Isaiah 14:9-11)

Along with Satan, the Bible states that the evil angels who were in allegiance with him are locked up in chains with him:

"For if God did not spare the angels when they sinned, but cast them deep into Hell, placing them in chains of darkness to be held for Judgment;" (2 Peter 2:4), "and the angels who did not stay within their own domain but abandoned their proper dwelling— these He has kept in eternal chains under darkness, bound for Judgment on that Great Day." (Jude 1:6)

The defeated devil and his angels are taken to prison, where they await their trial. Satan, the originator of lies and violence, is stripped of his power and confined to a prison where he can no longer deceive the nations. They have a thousand years to reflect on where their lies and violence have led them. Their ability to deceive and conduct their destructive plans is eliminated during this time.

Prophecies indicate that the Earth will be desolate, with all the wicked having died due to the judgments poured upon it. If any had survived the Bowls of Wrath, they were consumed: *"The Lord will consume with the Breath of His Mouth and destroy with the Brightness of His Coming." (2 Thessalonians 2:8)*

HELL'S PROPHECY

The Prophet Isaiah saw this day and prophesied:

"How you have fallen from heaven, O Lucifer, son of the morning! How you are cut down to the ground, you who weakened the nations! Yet you shall be brought down to Sheol, to the lowest depths of the Pit." (Isaiah 14:12)

It was tragic for the highest angel in heaven to think he was superior to the One who Created him. We receive information about what was in the deranged angel's thinking:

"Because your heart is lifted, and you say, 'I am a god, I sit in the seat of gods, in the midst of the seas,' yet you are a man, and not a god, though you set your heart as the heart of a god..."(Ezekiel 28:2) saying, *"I will ascend into heaven, I will exalt my throne above the stars of God; ...I will ascend above the heights of the clouds, I will be like the Most High."(Isaiah 14:13-14)*

Yahweh speaks more on Satan's delusion:

"You were the seal of perfection, full of wisdom and perfect in beauty. You were in Eden, the garden of God. Every kind of precious stone adorned you: ruby, topaz, and diamond, beryl, onyx, and jasper, sapphire, turquoise, and emerald. Your mountings and settings were crafted in gold and prepared on the day of your creation.

You were anointed as a guardian cherub, for I had ordained you. You were on Yahweh's Holy Mountain; you walked among the fiery stones. You were perfect in your ways from the day you were created till iniquity was found in you." (Ezekiel 28:12-15)

The thousand-year prison sentence has ended:

"And when the thousand years shall have been completed, Satan will be released out of his prison." At the same time: *"The*

sea gave up its dead, and Death and Hades gave up their dead" (Revelation 20:13).

Satan the Liar goes *"out to deceive the nations in the four corners of the earth—Gog and Magog—to assemble them for battle. Their number is like the sand of the seashore."* (Revelation 20:8)

Now Satan is let out of prison, and the wicked followers are raised in the second resurrection: *"The rest of the dead(wicked) did not come to life until the thousand years were ended."* (Revelation 20:5). Of course, the Author of evil had a thousand years to contrive a plan on what to do when he was released from his "jail cell." It is time to see the Judge for sentencing. He is not heading that way by himself. Now Satan goes with his deceived:

"And they marched across the broad expanse of the earth and surrounded the camp of the saints and the Beloved City." (Revelation 20:8,9)

The Devil's strategy: Deceive all of the wicked resurrected to believe that the massive amount of wicked folks (Billions of them) can run up and overtake New Jerusalem. Little does the wicked realize that the Old Serpent leads the masses straight to the Judgment scene. The Revelator describes it this way:

"And I saw the dead, great and small, standing before the Throne. Books were opened, and one of them was the Book of Life. And the dead were judged according to their deeds, as recorded in the books." (Revelation 20:12)

Those whom Satan has led to Yahweh's Courtroom now gaze at Lucifer and recognize how misled they had been in following this Master of disaster. Thus, the fulfillment of the Prophet

Isaiah, who beheld Satan's downfall and the sarcasm of those he deceived.

Your heart was lifted up because of your beauty; you corrupted your wisdom for the sake of your splendor. I cast you to the ground, I laid you before kings, that they might gaze at you...Those who see you will stare at you and consider you, saying: 'Is this the man who made the Earth tremble, who shook kingdoms, who made the world a wilderness and destroyed its cities, who did not open the house of his prisoners? (Ezekiel 28:17; Isaiah 14:15-17)

The wicked resurrected asked, "Are you the Big Man now, Little Satan? Are you the one who demanded homage and worship? Why did you lie to us? Why did you promise the world would be at our command if we followed your path? You Devil? If you have the power and authority you claim, get us out of this mess."

It is way too late now. They are trapped together, awaiting their turn to see the Judge on His Great White Throne. The prophecy continues:

"You are cast out of your grave Like an abominable branch, like the garment of those who are slain, thrust through with a sword, who go down to the stones of the pit, like a corpse trodden underfoot. You will not be joined with them in burial because you have destroyed your land and slain your people. The brood of evildoers shall never be." (Isaiah 14:18-20)

Prepare a place of slaughter for his sons because of the wrongdoing of their fathers. They must not arise, take possession of the Earth, and fill the world's surface with cities. This is the purpose proposed against the whole Earth, and this is the Hand stretched out over all the nations. For Yahweh of Hosts has purposed, and who will annul it? His Hand is stretched out, and who will turn it back?" (Isaiah 14:21,26,27)

One by one, those who had rejected the truth and lived the lies step up to the Judgment Seat. The Books are opened: the Book of Words, the Book of Works, and the Book of Life. As the Righteous Judge Yahweh deems the offender guilty, He pronounces the sentence of execution.

The Mighty Angels who participated in the 'round-up' seize the person who screams and gnashes their teeth and cast them into the "Lake of Fire," where they die a second and final time. Fire comes down from heaven and devours them. It rains so fast and hard that a lake instantly appears on Earth. No one can stop Yahweh's unquenchable fire as it burns and consumes the evildoers.

Finally, the prophecy concerning the Rebellious Angel and the Originator of evil stands fulfilled before the One who comes last—Satan Himself. The devil, along with the evil angels who rebelled with him, bows their knees and confesses to the Almighty that, indeed, Yeshua is above all names. It is written:

"And the devil who had deceived them, was thrown into the Lake of Fire and sulfur, into which the beast and the false prophet had already been thrown." (Revelation 20:10)

The prophet Daniel, 2,500 years ago, concerning this time of Judgment and observing the same thing, declared:

"I watched till the beast was slain, and its body destroyed and given to the burning flame." (Daniel 7:11).

The Beast and the False Prophet, who deceived the world by enforcing the Mark of the Beast, were thrown into the fire, devoured, and destroyed.

HELL'S PROPHECY

Speaking of Satan through the Prophet Ezekiel, we are provided a clearer picture of the exact punishment that Yahweh determined for his end:

"Therefore, I brought fire from your midst; it devoured you, and I turned you to ashes upon the Earth in the sight of all who saw you. All who knew you among the peoples are astonished at you; you have become a horror and shall be no more forever." (Ezekiel 28:16-19)

From the beginning of the Rebellion, the Father and the Son, through the Spirit, had prepared a special place to eliminate the Devil, his angels, and all evildoers. With frightening words, Yeshua announces:

"Depart from Me; you cursed, into the everlasting fire prepared for the devil and his angels." (Matthew 25:41)

Yes, upon the Earth, not underneath it, Yahweh's consuming fire engulfs the horror and terror-maker. All the unfallen world, who knew the wiles of the Devil and how he influenced the whole world, is astonished as the Fire and Sulfur devour the last link to evil, turning him to ashes before everyone's eyes. Now, he is **"no more forever."**

To be "no more forever" after Satan is turned to ashes suggests that the devil will not be the punisher, but one of the punished. The last enemy to be destroyed is death – the death of the wicked and the originator of evil: they are no more. It is the end of the matter.

Yeshua's work to destroy Satan has been completed. The devil meets the fire that produces the everlasting effect of being turned to ashes. When the Fire came, it was unquenchable. Not even Satan could stop it.

So – Are You Facing Bad News?

The prophet Isaiah asked this question about the fire:

"Who among us shall dwell with the devouring fire? Who among us shall dwell with everlasting burnings?" (Isaiah 33:14). "For it is the Day of Yahweh's Vengeance... its streams shall be turned into pitch, and its dust into brimstone, its land shall become burning pitch; it shall not be put out night or day, its smoke shall ascend forever" (Isaiah 34:9-10). "And the smoke of their torment will rise forever and ever." (Revelation 14:11)

This desolate portrait paints a picture of a Fire that devours everything. Who will be able to survive it? According to this vision, nothing will. The land will turn into burning pitch and brimstone. The only remaining evidence of the destruction will be the *smoke* continuously ascending into the atmosphere, serving as a perpetual reminder that evil has its consequences.

Let us understand the phrase "*unquenchable fire*" at this point. When Yahweh, through the prophet Jeremiah, warned Israel concerning Jerusalem of not regarding His Sabbath, they were warned:

"If you do not obey me to keep the Sabbath day holy by not carrying any load as you come through the gates of Jerusalem on the Sabbath day, I will kindle an unquenchable fire in the gate of Jerusalem that will consume her fortresses." (Jeremiah 17:27)

This prophecy met its fulfillment when Jerusalem fell to the Babylonians, as recorded in 2 Kings 25:8-10:

Nebuchadnezzar, king of Babylon, and Nebuzaradan, commander of the imperial guard and an official of the king of Babylon, came to Jerusalem. He set fire to the Temple of Yahweh,

HELL'S PROPHECY

the Royal Palace, and all the houses of Jerusalem. Every important building he burned down."

Because the people of Jerusalem did not heed Yahweh's warning, the Babylonian King invaded Jerusalem and burned down Jerusalem with *unquenchable fire*. Even the world's most excellent fire department would be unable to quench this fire sent from the Almighty. The fire burned down everything - then it went out.

Oh, there is one more vital point to consider left. One other prophecy reveals a time afterward, as the smoke ascends into the atmosphere as a result of the burning, the only one thing left alive to do the cleanup is - the maggots:

"And they shall go forth and look upon the corpses of the men who have transgressed against me, for their worm does not die, and their fire is not quenched." (Isaiah 66:24).

Imagine a worm feeding on a dead body, sustained by a never-ending feast, with an unlimited supply of corpses to consume. An annihilating fire burns the bodies, while the *"undying worm"* will have plenty to feast on for a long time.

The maggots are eating corpses—not *the living dead*. Once they have cleaned up the mess of dead bodies, the worms will be so fat that they will at least want to die - you think?

No, the wicked do not live on forever. They will perish, vanish, be eternally destroyed, cut off, burned up, consumed, uprooted, plucked up, devoured, go up in smoke, turn to ashes, and be no more forever.

So, what is the verdict? Is there such a thing as eternal conscious torment in Hell? No.

So – Are You Facing Bad News?

As we are all aware that one day, we will leave this life and be buried beneath the ground we now walk on. There is no escaping this stark reality. The Scriptures tell us that a specific portion of time is allocated to each of us:

"The days of our lives are seventy years; and if, because of strength, they are eighty years, yet their boast is only labor and sorrow; for it is soon cut off, and we fly away." (Psalm 90:10)

And then, the Bible writer concludes with this prayer:

"So, teach us to number our days, that we may gain a heart of wisdom." (Psalm 90:12)

The bottom line: We all will die. Some will live a little longer than others in the allotted time. As we gain the courage to face this certainty of an end, we are admonished with these wise words:

"However, anyone may live for many years, and let them enjoy them all. But let them remember the days of darkness, for there will be many. Everything to come is meaningless. You who are young, be happy while you are young, and let your heart give you joy in the days of your youth. Follow the ways of your heart and whatever your eyes see, but know that God will bring you into Judgment for all these things." (Ecclesiastes 11:8-9)

There will be some good days—and there will be some bad ones. The days are heading to a dead end. Therefore, enjoy each day your Creator grants you—and be careful how you live on this Earth. The wise man again instructs us:

HELL'S PROPHECY

"Don't let the excitement of being young cause you to forget about your Creator. Honor Him in your youth before the evil years come—when you'll no longer enjoy living. It will be too late to remember Him when the sun, light, moon, and stars are dim to your old eyes, and no silver lining is left among your clouds. There will come a time when your limbs will tremble with age, your strong legs will become weak, your teeth will be too few to do their work, and there will be blindness, too." (Ecclesiastes 12:1-3 TLB)

Then, let your lips be tightly closed while eating when your teeth are gone! You will wake at dawn with the first note of the birds, but you will be deaf and tuneless, with a quavering voice. You will be afraid of heights and of falling—a white-haired, withered older man, dragging himself along without sexual desire, standing at death's door, and nearing his everlasting home as the mourners pass by." (Ecclesiastes 12:4-5 TLB)

What a profound insight into the truth regarding the aging process. The imagery of life presented here as we age may seem dismal: Eventually, our eyes can hardly see, our bodies shake, our legs cannot walk very far, our teeth rot and fall out, and we cannot hear anything without hearing aids, no longer able to carry a tune, afraid of ladders, white-haired and withered, no longer interested in sex, standing at death's door. Wow!

I'm not sure about you, but this is sobering news! Ready or not—it will come. So, while we can still enjoy the years of our mobility and youthfulness, let us remember that we have a Creator over us who loves us and wants to guide our lives in blessings.

Time is ticking away swiftly. This short time on Earth can be disconcerting. One Bible writer illustrates our brevity this way:

So – Are You Facing Bad News?

You do not even know what will happen tomorrow! What is your life? You are a mist that appears for a little while and then vanishes. (James 4:14)

While you are still able to comprehend and reflect on your existence, make sure that you understand this:

"You never know when your time is coming. Like birds suddenly caught in a trap, like fish caught in a net, we are trapped at some evil moment when we least expect it." (Ecclesiastes 9:11-12 GNT)

Over and over in Scripture, we are reminded to walk in awareness of this profound truth:

"A wise man's heart discerns both time and Judgment because, for every matter, there is a time and Judgment, though man's misery increases significantly. For he does not know what will happen, so who can tell him when it will occur? No one has power over the Spirit to retain the Spirit, and no one has power on the day of death. (Ecclesiastes 8:5-8)

How many of us have experienced this shocking truth? One day, we hear of someone we know who wakes up having their day planned out, and the next moment, they are hanging on to life in an emergency room. Thousands of people visit the ER every day. Some make it out, while others never make it out alive. Very few can predict what one day will bring. Calamity is indiscriminate.

One evening, a church friend stayed the night at our house. Her husband had just died of an unexpected cancer that killed him in less than a month. She was moving to a new home to start a new life without him. That evening, she discussed how a new coat of paint and remodeling would transform her new abode into a "doll house." She was eager to start her new life, putting the recent tragedy behind her.

The following day, she left our house around 5:30 a.m., heading to her new home, which was a few hours away. We received a phone call from an emergency room later that morning with the tragic news - she had been murdered. We have no idea what one day will bring. Life is uncertain. We are here one minute - gone the next. The Bible tells us all about it.

How many friends or loved ones have you lost suddenly? Yes, we must face uncertainty. While we are yet cognitively able to understand these Scriptural realities and apply them in our lives, there is no moment to waste. Time is short and getting shorter. If we know where our lives will end up, why not take it seriously and prepare for the unexpected?

As we contemplate uncertainty, it would also be well for us to understand the certainties of life:

"For there is not a just man on Earth who does good and does not sin." (Ecclesiastes 7:20)

As good as we think we may be, the wise man says our goodness falls short of the mark. When someone is born into the world, they inherit a sinful nature. Many good-hearted people do many kind acts to others, but in God's Sight:

"All of us have become like one who is unclean, and all our righteous acts are like filthy rags; we all shrivel up like a leaf, and like the wind, our sins sweep us away." (Isaiah 64:6)

No matter how clean our lives appear, a stain has seeped into our clothes through sin, and our efforts to clean them up are futile. Once a person breaks the Creator's Law in rebellion against Him, according to the Bible, we become disconnected:

"Your iniquities have separated you from your God, and your sins have hidden His Face from you - so that He will not hear." (Isaiah 59:2)

The bottom line is that our sin separates us from our relationship with God. There is no possible way to fix what has been broken on our own. When our first parents sinned, we inherited their sinful nature:

"Therefore, just as sin entered the world through one man, and death through sin, so also death was passed on to all men because all sinned. (Romans 5:12)

Because of this, humanity is in deep trouble spiritually:

"As for you, you were dead in your transgressions and sins, in which you used to live when you followed the ways of this world and the ruler of the kingdom of the air, the spirit who is now at work in those who are disobedient. All of us also lived among them at one time, gratifying the cravings of our flesh and following its desires and thoughts. Like the rest, we were by nature deserving of wrath." (Ephesians 2:1-3)

At one time, we, too, were foolish, disobedient, misled, and enslaved to all sorts of desires and pleasures—living in malice and envy, being hated, and hating one another. (Titus 3:3)

Based on these shocking truths, we are controlled by a spirit led by an evil influencer. Without help from God, we are walking, talking dead folks. We have no way to prevent the desires of our sinful nature from overtaking us in our own efforts. We are just plain helpless:

"For the flesh craves what is contrary to the Spirit, and the Spirit what is contrary to the flesh. They are opposed to each other so that you do not do what you want." (Galatians 5:17)

Continually, in the Scriptures, we are forewarned that things in our lives need to change to enter the Kingdom of God. It is imperative to get control over the passions and lust that control our hearts and emotions. Here is one such warning:

"Put to death, therefore, the components of your earthly nature: sexual immorality, impurity, lust, evil desires, and greed, which is idolatry. Because of these, the Wrath of God is coming on the sons of disobedience." (Colossians 3:5-7)

We have learned that there is a payday for sin. Death and God's Wrath are coming to those who are rebellious and self-centered. Count on it. Many live "blowing and going" without considering where these unrestrained passions will lead them. Here is where it is all heading:

"It is appointed for men to die once, but after this the Judgment." (Hebrews 9:27)

We can discern some harsh realities based on the truths revealed in these testimonies. We have just a short time on this Earth to find our way. Our Creator sets parameters for us to live within. We are alerted to the fact that:

"When you follow the desires of your sinful nature, the results are obvious: sexual immorality, impurity, lustful pleasures, idolatry, sorcery, hostility, quarreling, jealousy, outbursts of anger, selfish ambition, dissension, division, envy, drunkenness, wild parties, and other sins like these. Let me tell you again, as I have before, that anyone living that sort of life will not inherit the Kingdom of God." (Galatians 5:19-21)

So – Are You Facing Bad News?

So: *"Let us hear the conclusion of the whole matter: Fear Yahweh and keep His Commandments, for this is man's all. For Yahweh will bring every work into Judgment, including every secret thing, whether good or evil." (Ecclesiastes 12:13-14)*

Because of man's sin, death will fall on all of us—make no mistake. But this is not "the final answer." One day, we must answer for our rebellion on a day when:

"God will Judge the secrets of mankind through Christ Jesus." (Romans 2:6)

First, we must realize our need for change, that our paths lead to eternal destruction, and that we cannot measure up or fix what is broken. The good news is that there is a way up and out of the ball and chains we are wrapped up in. It starts with a weighty introspection of our hearts.

It is time to hear some good news about these harsh realities. Yes, God has provided us with a way of escape and freedom from sin and death. He never intended for us to stray and leave our relationship with Him. There is a way to break loose from the Judgment of the Second Death and come clean with our Maker. It does not cost you a penny!

Hell, With the Good News

"God demonstrated His Love for us, in that while we were still sinners, Christ died for us."

-Romans 5:8

If we are left with the bad news of imminent death and Judgment without a remedy, we will stay in despair and hopelessness. Sometimes, the realization of crises awakens us to the need to search for solutions. Unfortunately, the grim news must be recognized first. If we do not see our deplorable condition, we will not feel the need to change it.

We must recognize the absolute truth concerning the bad news about our actual condition and an inevitable future:

1) We, on our own ability, have no power over our sinful natures to keep from sinning and offending God.

2) Because of rebellion against our Creator, death will eventually overtake us.

3) There will be an appointed time set for us to see the Judge as we come out of our graves to receive our reward for accepting or rejecting the truth.

4) The time to choose and turn our lives around so that we can walk in the freedom of Grace is short and unpredictable.

5) To enter God's Kingdom, we must change our hearts and take definite action to rid ourselves of the weight of bad decisions and actions that bring on accountability and sentencing before the Judge of the whole Earth.

6) Once Judged and without representation when the Court is set, the offender will die again – a Second Death in a Fire that will consume its recipients.

7) Eternal condemnation brings eternal fire, resulting in everlasting destruction and irreversible death. Destroyed, perished, and cut off from eternal life.

Friends, we are not left to lousy news without a way to escape from it. Announcing Good News: A Savior was sent to resolve, reconcile, and repair the broken bond between humanity and their Creator. Here is the Gospel:

"God So Loved the world that He gave His One and Only Son that everyone who believes in Him should not perish but have eternal life. For God did not send his Son into the world to condemn the world, but that the world should be saved through Him." (John 3:16-17)

As broken as humanity had become, our loving Creator took this into His Own Hands, providing His only Son to die, paying off the penalty for our sins. Because of His Love and Grace, He has not left us without hope and a solution. God SO LOVED you that He gave up His most prized possession: His Only Son.

It was not in Yahweh's Heart to condemn us but to rescue us from sin's power and authority over us. Man's restoration could come only one way:

"God made the One who knew no sin to be sin for us so that in Him we would become the righteousness of God." (2 Corinthians 5:21)

Because God is Holy, He would only accept a sinless sacrifice. He gave up Jesus:

"who committed no sin, nor was deceit found in His Mouth; who, when He was reviled, did not revile in return; when He

HELL'S PROPHECY

Suffered, He did not threaten, but committed Himself to Him who Judges Righteously; who Himself bore our sins in His Own Body on the tree, that we having died to sins, might live for righteousness— by whose stripes you were healed." (1 Peter 2:22-24)

Yeshua came down from heaven to save and heal the lost. He demonstrated His Love for humanity as He prophesied His intent:

"Greater love has no one than this than to lay down one's life for his friends." (John 15:13)

At the appointed time, just before His Death, Jesus proclaimed:

"Father, the hour has come. Glorify Your Son, that Your Son also may Glorify You, as You have given Him Authority over all flesh, that He should give Eternal Life to as many as You have given Him. And this is Eternal Life, that they may know You, the Only True God, and Jesus Christ whom You have sent. I have glorified You on the Earth. I have finished the work which You have given Me. And now, O Father, Glorify Me with Yourself, with the Glory I had with You before the world was." (John 17:1-5)

Now, the time had come to finish the work He came to accomplish—to take on the sins and penalties of those He loved. The mission was clear:

"Yeshua Messiah came into the world to save sinners."

(1 Timothy 1:15)

So, do we need saving? To restore His Prized Creation, Jesus had to die and pay the penalty pronounced upon humanity's first parents in the Garden of Eden. When Adam disobeyed God's order, he sinned, and death was passed on to all who would live afterward: *"For as in Adam all die." (1 Corinthians 15:22)*

Hell, With the Good News

The decision had been made to provide a substitute for our death sentence. But death could not contain the Messiah, who laid down His Life willfully and was raised from the grave for our justification:

"For since death came through a man, the Resurrection of the dead comes also through a Man. As in Adam all die, so in Yeshua all will be made alive." (1 Corinthians 15:21-22)

History testifies that Jesus was condemned as a criminal and died a criminal's worst death by crucifixion. After He died, they took the precious Son of God off the cross and placed Him in a sealed tomb; some of His followers returned three days later to the burial site only to find the stone had been rolled away. The testimony of truth revealed:

"But they found the stone rolled away from the tomb. Then, they went in and did not find the Body of the Lord Jesus. And it happened, as they were greatly perplexed about this, two men stood by them in shining garments. As they were afraid and bowed their faces to the Earth, they said to them, 'Why do you seek the living among the dead? He is not here, but HE HAS RISEN!"

(Luke 24:2-6)

The Resurrection of Yeshua is an irrefutable fact of history, supported by firsthand eyewitnesses. One eyewitness declares:

"That which was from the beginning, which we have heard, which we have seen with our own eyes, which we have gazed upon and touched with our own hands—this is the Word of Life. And this is the Life that was revealed; we have seen it and testified to it, and we proclaim to you the Eternal Life that was with the Father and was revealed to us. We proclaim to you what we have seen and heard..." (1 John 1:1-3)

One eyewitness of history proclaims:

"For I delivered to you first of all that which I also received: that Christ died for our sins according to the Scriptures, and that He was buried, and that He rose again the Third Day according to the Scriptures." (1 Corinthians 15:3-4)

This is not the testimony of just one witness. Paul, one of those who also encountered the Risen Savior, proclaims Jesus:

"Was seen by Cephus, then by the twelve. After that, He was seen by over five hundred brethren at once, of whom the greater part remain to the present, but some have fallen asleep. After that, He was seen by James, then by all the Apostles. Then, last of all, I also saw him." (1 Corinthians 15:5-8)

In addition, Luke, the historian, adds that Jesus was with His followers and seen after the Resurrection for forty days:

"Until the day in which He was taken up, after He through the Holy Spirit had given Commandments to the Apostles whom He had chosen, to whom He also presented Himself Alive after His suffering by many infallible proofs, being seen by them during forty days and speaking of the things about the Kingdom of God." (Acts 1:2-3)

Another Eyewitness attests to the truth of the Resurrection:

"Now, in these Last Days, He has spoken to us by His Son, whom He had appointed Heir of all things, through whom also He made the Worlds; who being the Brightness of His Glory and the Express Image of His Person, and upholding all things by the Word of His Power, when He had by Himself purged our sins, sat down at the Right Hand of the Majesty on High." (Hebrews 1:2-3)

Because of the eyewitnesses to the story of Yeshua's Resurrection, we have hope and the promise of eternal life. My book and your faith would be in vain if He had not been raised from the dead. We are not following myths or legends here. We can rely on the numerous faithful testimonies throughout history. His Story!

The Apostle Peter, a disciple and devout follower of Yeshua, boldly asserted:

"For we did not follow cleverly devised stories when we told you about the Coming of our Lord Jesus Christ in Power, but we were eyewitnesses of His Majesty. He received Honor and Glory from God the Father when the Voice came to Him from the Majestic Glory, saying, "This is my Son, whom I love; with Him I am well pleased." We heard this Voice that came from Heaven when we were with Him on the Sacred Mountain."

(2 Peter 2:16-18)

Peter sealed his testimony in blood. When he was given the chance to recant his story or die, he refused and was beaten without mercy and eventually crucified upside down for the truth. The early church fathers are unanimous in claiming that Peter died in Rome by crucifixion during the persecution of Nero in AD 64.[28]

Although we were not present when the Messiah appeared as a Man of history, we have many reliable sources who were eyewitnesses to Yeshua's claims of being God, the Miracles that backed up His Words, and faithful servants who were there in His Day to testify that He lived a sinless Life. The sealing cap of all truth came when Yeshua Rose from the grave with Victory over death.

John sums up our hope with this profound statement:

"And this is the Testimony: God has given us eternal life, and this life is in His Son. Whoever has the Son has life; whoever does not have the Son of God does not have life. I write these things to

you who believe in the Name of the Son of God so that you may know that you have eternal life." (1 John 5:11-13)

The bad news must be set aside for the Good News of the truth—that our Creator and Savior have made provisions for us to choose our path from here. Faith is not blind. Based on historical attestation from eyewitnesses, we can conclude that God SO loved us; His Son died and was raised back to life to bring hope to the hopeless and reconcile humanity that was lost back into a relationship with Himself.

We are not saved from the wrath to come on our own merits. Salvation is offered to us as a free gift:

"For it is by grace you have been saved, through faith—and this is not from yourselves, it is the gift of God." (Ephesians 2:8)

The gift is there for you to take. If you're facing bad news, turn around and chase after the good news. Believe it, take it to heart, walk in it, and then stand in the evil day with the Promise of a Faithful Savior who assures us:

"I will never leave you or forsake you..." (Hebrews 13:5)

Here Is the Best News

"Truly, I say to you, he who hears My Word and believes in Him who sent Me has everlasting life and shall not come into judgment but has passed from death into life."

-John 5:24

I admit that some of the themes in this book will cause anxiety and alarm. However, I assure you that following the Bible's prescribed path will benefit your soul and bring you peace with your Maker.

Yeshua promises us that if we hear and pay attention to His Words, we can count on three things:

1) Eternal Life
2) No Judgment
3) Pass from death to life

The wages of sin usher us to death, but God's gift is eternal life in Yeshua the Messiah (Romans 6:23). He deeply desires to give it to us.

There is also assurance that we will not be judged, which will result in experiencing a Second Death. We will leap into an abundant life that starts now, with no waiting for eternity to have God's Plan initiated in the present:

"For I know the plans I have for you," declares Yahweh, *"plans to prosper you and not to harm you, plans to give you hope and a future." (Jeremiah 29:11)*

So, what does God require of us? Here it is:

"For as many as received Him, to them He gave the right to become children of God, to those who believe in His Name." (John 1:12)

To become a child of the Most High God, you must *receive* Him. This means that you must let Him become the Lord of your life. To be "Lord" means to be "Ruler" over your life. Jesus implores:

"Look at me. I stand at the door. I knock. If you hear Me call and open the door, I will come right in and sit down to supper with you." (Revelation 3:20)

To *receive* the Savior, you must first recognize His Voice calling you. He is standing outside your heart's door and knocking for a way to get in. The doorknob is on the inside. When you open, he will establish His Relationship with you.

To *believe* means He died to save you from your sin. Be honest with yourself and God, and He will forgive you if you ask Him:

"If we confess our sins, He is faithful and just to forgive us and cleanse us from all unrighteousness. (1 John 1:9)

When you do this, He is faithful to deliver on His promises:

"He has not dealt with us according to our sins nor punished us according to our iniquities. As the Heavens are high above the Earth, so great is His Mercy toward those who fear Him; as far as the East is from the West, so far has He removed our transgressions from us. As a father pities his children, Yahweh pities those who fear Him." (Psalm 103:10-14)

"Who is a God like You, pardoning iniquity and passing over the transgression of the remnant of His Heritage? He does not

retain His Anger forever because He delights in Mercy. He will again have compassion for us and will subdue our iniquities. You will cast all our sins into the depths of the sea." (Micah 7:18-19)

When you believe in your heart, the truth - confess it:

"If you confess with your mouth the Lord Jesus and believe in your heart that God has raised Him from the dead, you will be saved. For with the heart, one believes unto righteousness, and with the mouth, confession is made unto salvation. The Scripture says, 'Whoever believes in Him will not be put to shame." (Romans 10:9-10)

Friends, I will end this Book by reflecting on my unsaved Mother. I accept that my mom chose to walk on the path she decided would give her happiness. There is no reversing the order of things now. To realize that my loss is eternal will be heartbreaking until the day that I close my eyes to the sleep of death. But even in this stark reality, I am much more comforted to know that Mom will not be tortured and agonized in some Fire Pit throughout the eternal ages. In the Judgment, she will perish in the Second Death. Gone forever... So:

"God grant me the serenity to accept the things I cannot change, the courage to change the things I can, and the wisdom to know the difference." [27]

Reinhold Niebuhr

Friends, there are two paths that you can walk on. One leads to eternal life; the other leads to a Second Death. While you can read my plea and appeal, if you are on the wrong path, there is still time to change it. Just turn around your way and do it correctly; it is called "repentance." Your way does not work well.

HELL'S PROPHECY

"And the Spirit and the Bride say, 'Come!' And let him who hears say, 'Come!' And let him who thirsts come. Whoever desires, let him take the Water of Life freely." (Revelation 22:17)

Have things not been going as planned for you? What do you place your hope on? What shall benefit you if the whole world is gained, yet you lose your soul in pursuing it all? What will you offer in exchange for your soul? The Spirit calls you to *Come* and find the rest you have desperately been searching for. The Merciful Savior invites us:

"Are you tired? Worn out? Burned out on religion? Come to Me. Get away with me, and you will recover your life. I will show you how to take a real rest. Walk with me and work with me—watch how I do it. Learn the unforced rhythms of grace. I will not lay anything heavy or ill-fitting on you. Keep company with me, and you will learn to live freely and lightly." (Matthew 11:28-30 MSG)

Do this, and you will find rest in your souls. This is the truth and nothing but the truth – so help me, God.

About the Author

Over thirty-five years ago, Steve Henderson left the darkness behind and began experiencing the joy of knowing his Creator intimately. He heard a message of love, mercy, and forgiveness and embraced the opportunity for a relationship with God. Since then, his journey has been fascinating.

Steve searched deeply for life's truths and began reading the Bible. Through extensive research, he discovered that the Bible is historically accurate, archaeologically verified, and prophetically confirmed. Compelled by this evidence, he responded to the Great Invitation.

Steve was captivated by Jesus's teachings. Jesus did not just preach about love; He embodied it in every aspect of His life. His teachings are solid, His life is a living testament to His words, and His offer is incredibly compelling. Islam recognizes Jesus as a true prophet; some see Him as a great teacher, and everyone acknowledges His extraordinary nature.

Jesus made astonishing claims about His identity that left many people baffled. He boldly stated, *"I am the Way, the Truth, and the Life."* As Steve delved deeper into his research, he realized the extraordinary nature of these claims. Imagine someone today declaring they are God; most would think they are out of their mind. Steve concluded that Jesus was either delusional, dishonest, or the embodiment of Truth.

Everything Jesus proclaimed before His death was confirmed by historical eyewitnesses who testified to His Resurrection. Historians affirm that Jesus rose from His grave just as the prophets had foretold. This historical testimony solidified everything Jesus taught about eternal life as Steve's guiding truth, his study, and his pursuit.

When committing to this life-changing path, Steve worked as a bartender. He decided to trade serving drinks for sharing the gospel. Jesus offered him hope and a solid doctrine that transformed his life. Now, Steve strives to reflect God's Love to everyone he meets and shares an incredible story of God's Amazing Grace.

Over the past few decades, Steve has devoted himself to various facets of ministry, driven by a passion for guiding and supporting others on their spiritual journeys. His formal journey began with a seminary program in the Denver, Colorado, area, which laid the foundation for his ministerial work.

For six years, Steve served as the pastor of a dynamic church in Kansas City, Missouri, where he led a vibrant congregation. He then founded "The Pastor's Helper," a ministry dedicated to equipping the church for its vital work. Through this ministry, he conducted seminars in Evangelism, Discipleship, Leadership Training, Spiritual Gifts, Apologetics, and Bible Prophecy.

Steve is also the founder of Sure Word of Prophecy Ministries (www.surewordprophecy.org), where he creates videos to help atheists and agnostics understand the Omniscient Nature of the Creator, who knows the end from the beginning. Additionally, he owns the Bible Prophecy Connection on LinkedIn, where he moderates a group of enthusiasts interested in Bible prophecy.

In addition to these endeavors, Steve is deeply involved in prison ministry with Prison Fellowship, teaching and mentoring inmates in Oklahoma prisons.

Reference

1) Mary Baxter - *A Divine Revelation of Hell - Chapter 3*
2) *Hank Hanegraaff, Bible Answer Man Radio Program, June 16, 2009.* https://www.equip.org/hank_speaks_out/the-existence-of-hell/#:~:text=Common%20sense%20also%20dictates%20that,Christian%20Research%20Journal%20on%20hell.
3) David Nichols's Article (Blog) entitled Hell, April 18th, 2012 https://atheistfoundation.org.au/2012/04/hell-2/
4) - C.S., "The Problem of Pain" Collier Books/Macmillan Publishing Company, New York, NY 1962, p. 119
5) Ezekiel 33:11
6) *"A Divine Revelation of Hell" Mary Baxter Chapter 2*
7) *Quote by Carl Sandburg* http://www.vn.thinkexist.com/quotes/with/keyword/die_hard/
8) *Barnhart, Robert K. (1995). The Barnhart Concise Dictionary of Etymology, page 348. HarperCollins ISBN 0-06-270084-7*
9) https://www.encyclopedia.com/philosophy-and-religion/other-religious-beliefs-and-general-terms/religion-general/
10) *The Divine Comedy of Dante Alighieri. The Italian Text with a Translation in English Blank Verse and a*

HELL'S PROPHECY

Commentary by Courtney Langdon, vol. 1 (Inferno) (Cambridge: Harvard University Press, 1918). English version.
https://www.dentonisd.org/cms/lib/TX21000245/Centricity/Domain/982/inferno%203.pdf

11) Robert Anton Wilson, "Cheerful Reflections on Death and Dying," Gnoware, February 1999
https://www.tapatalk.com/groups/mountbiblicalsense/thoughts-on-everlasting-punishment-t1504033.html

12) *-Sermons 1. 72 (Translated by Rev. Orby Shipley)*

13) *- Article V, Universal Declaration of Human Rights - U.N. General Assembly, December 10, 1948*

14) *In Furman v. Georgia, the United States Supreme Court*

15) *Convention (III) concerning the Treatment of Prisoners of War. Geneva, 12 August 1949.*

16) *, c. 200 Mark Minucius Felix*

17) *Reverend J. Furniss, C.S.S.R in his book The Sight of Hell (A Catholic book for children)*

18) *Jonathan Edwards, "The Eternity of Hell Torments," The Wrath of Almighty God. (Morgan, PA: Soli Deo Gloria Publications, 1996), 356-7.*

19) *Stephen Travels -Top 5 Depictions of Hell*
https://stephentravels.com/top5/depictions-of-hell/

20) *Poems, 1799 by Robert Southey, page 36 of 147*

21) *Mary Baxter A Divine Revelation of Hell Chapter Two - The Left Leg of Hell*

22) *Bill Weise 23 Minutes in Hell Chapter 3 The Gateway Published by Charisma House*

Reference

23) *Mary Baxter A Divine Revelation of Hell Chapter 2*

24) *Bill Weise 23 Minutes in Hell*

25) *Merriam-Webster Dictionary - definition of death*

26) *23 Minutes in Hell P.107*

27) *Niebuhr, Reinhold (September 10, 1987). Brown, Robert McAfee (ed.). The Essential Reinhold Niebuhr: Selected Essays and Addresses (New ed.). Yale University Press. p. 251*

28) *https://evidenceforchristianity.org/what-is-the-evidence-that-peter-was-crucified-upside-down-in-rome/*

www.ingramcontent.com/pod-product-compliance
Lightning Source LLC
Chambersburg PA
CBHW031356040426
42444CB00005B/312